WITHDRAWN

Customer is King

How to Exceed Their Expectations

Robert Craven

This edition first published in Great Britain in 2005 by
Virgin Books Ltd
Thames Wharf Studios
Rainville Road
London
W6 9HA

First published in 2002 by Virgin Books Ltd

6 7 8 9 10

A catalogue record for this book is available from the British Library.

ISBN 978 0 7535 0968 5

Series Consultant: Professor David Storey
Joint Series Editors: Robert Craven, Grier Palmer

The Random House Group Limited supports The Forest Stewardship
Council (FSC), the leading international forest certification organisation.
All our titles that are printed on Greenpeace approved FSC certified paper
carry the FSC logo. Our paper procurement policy can be found at:
www.rbooks.co.uk/environment

MIX
Paper from
responsible sources
FSC® C013604

Series design by Janice Mather at Ben Cracknell Studios
Typeset by Phoenix Photosetting, Chatham, Kent
Printed and bound in Great Britain by CPI Antony Rowe, Chippenham, Wiltshire

To Cal, Jessie, Bonnie and Ben

Contents

Foreword
by Sir Richard Branson

I have always learnt my business on the job – from setting up *Student* magazine way back in 1967 right through to running the Virgin Group in the twenty-first century as one of the biggest brands in the world – rather than from a book, which makes it novel to be writing this foreword for the new editions of the Virgin Business Guide series.

I wouldn't call myself a marketing expert or a finance professional, however, nor am I the best person to do each and every job in the company – that's what I employ great staff for! And on a day-to-day basis, whatever the size of your company, you'll probably have advisers for all aspects of your business – from planning your next move to marketing and PR; from finance to problem solving and how to look after your customers – and these advisers are essential. At Virgin I do believe it is *my* job, though, to make the best possible decisions and that is only feasible if I know enough about each aspect of my business to make informed choices.

Learning from other people's business successes and failures can be an essential part of your own success. When I've experienced setbacks in my own business life, I have picked myself up again and had another go using the knowledge that I've gained from that failure. I have also always found advice from someone who's tried something similar before you – such as from Freddie Laker of Laker Airways when it came to running Virgin Atlantic and dealing with some of the early problems we encountered, or from Per

Lindstrand, who introduced me to ballooning and taught me much of what I know about it – one of the most important aspects of running my business. Even if, when it comes to it, I make my own decisions.

This series of books, in conjunction with Warwick Business School, is all written by businessmen and women who have been in business themselves and are therefore aware of the importance of information and the pitfalls you might come across. Not only that, but they include advice, ideas and case studies from many other successful and less successful businesspeople to help you.

In *Customer is King*, Robert Craven says that your 'whole business hinges on what your customer gets from you'. I agree wholeheartedly. Customers and customer service have long been essential to Virgin – from new customers to customers who have been with us for years – but, as every business should, we want to build on that. Whatever our official job titles, we all work in customer service.

The figures speak for themselves – about half of small businesses fail in the first four years – so in whatever industry you work you need all the help you can get to succeed. And, above all, you should be having fun. Use these books as your tools, follow the advice and then make your own decisions – after all, you're the boss!

Preface

Anyone who read Robert Craven's earlier book in the Virgin series, *Kick-Start Your Business*, will be familiar with his style. Robert does not provide a 'comfortable' read. Rather, he provokes the reader to undertake self-assessments in order to answer penetrating questions both about themselves and about their business. Perhaps, even more challengingly, Robert Craven demands the reader should then act upon the answers derived. In his view, and mine, if you require comfortable fiction, this book is not for you.

So how does this volume differ from *Kick-Start Your Business*? In my opinion, while *Kick-Start* provided the reader with an overview of their business, this one drills more deeply in one direction – marketing. But this is not a typical marketing book. Indeed, the book seems to delight in taking sideswipes at those whom Robert Craven views as making marketing more complex than it deserves to be – guilty parties include gurus, academics and, perhaps particularly, large-firm marketing directors.

So, if you run your own business, what simple guidance does the book supply? Robert Craven, who would be the first to recognise that this is certainly not rocket science, emphasises the importance of even the smallest firm seeking to differentiate itself in some way from the competition. Below are three examples of simple practice which is rarely practised

Example 1:   Your customers will nearly always tell you what they think of your product and service. They will tell you where it meets their requirements, where it fails to meet their requirements and where it exceeds their requirements. What is therefore so surprising is that so few firms actually ask their customers what they really think. So make sure you do.

Example 2: Dissatisfied customers can be the death knell of a business. Robert Craven reports the folklore research that businesses only know about four per cent of their dissatisfied customers. But what he points out is that, even when those dissatisfied customers make themselves known to the business, many get treated dismissively. As an aside I particularly recommend Robert's variation of the famous Monty Python 'dead parrot' sketch in Chapter 4.

Example 3: While most of us would recognise that it is difficult for smaller firms to benefit from being a brand, it is much easier for the firm to be special. If you wish to be special then Robert Craven provides a considerable number of ideas, particularly focusing upon how to enhance customer service.

This book will engage and challenge you, but it will not succeed in its ambitions unless it changes the way you run your business. There can be few business owners or managers that could fail to benefit from its ideas.

Professor David Storey
Director, Centre for Small and Medium Sized Enterprises
Warwick Business School, University of Warwick

Introduction

David Ogilvy pronounced that 'The customer is a moron'. Hmm . . .

As I was putting the finishing touches to this book, I went to one of my wife's staff parties. One of her friends asked me what the title of the new book was. When she heard that it was *Customer Is King*, her spontaneous reply was, 'Well, everyone knows what a con that is!' How right she is. But it doesn't have to be that way for you or for *your* customers.

This book does not contain a precise concept capable of being distilled into a neat one-liner. Instead, it describes a particular attitude and approach to business, a mindset, that will get you results. At the same time, the book is not prescriptive in its approach: it mixes up diagnosis, analysis, recommendations and strategies, because these things do not happen in a vacuum. Like a market stall, the book offers tips, techniques, advice, tools and templates that you can choose to use as appropriate to your situation

Customer Is King is all about having a clear understanding of what you are trying to do, and why and how you are going to do it. It will help you to become better than the competition and build stronger customer relationships.

The audience for this book includes anyone who is running his or her own business, or someone else's business. Whether you work alone or employ ten or a hundred and ten staff, the principles in this book will help your business to become more effective and more profitable, by focusing on the customer.

The audience for this work will also include people responsible for running an enterprise or for sales and marketing. If you have never quite bought into the awesome rhetoric of the marketing books (that bear so little relationship to life as we know it) then this book is for you.

Why this book?

My first book, *Kick-Start Your Business*, was about analysing the whole business – it was a springboard for sorting your business and how you run it. It was about deciding where you wanted to go and putting in place the processes and systems to make it happen.

Customer Is King is to some extent an extension of *Kick-Start*. The central belief in *Kick-Start* is that the really successful businesses are obsessed with three things: marketing, strategy and teams. I feel that the way that marketing has been delivered has been wrong. Somehow, the passion, the excitement and the rawness of finding and delighting customers has been theorised to death in the books. Whatever happened to the idea that a customer is like a friend and should be treated as such: with respect, warmth, care and compassion? Somewhere along the line, they seem to have lost the essential buzz and excitement that is around when you reach people who want to do business with you.

To get back in touch with the vitality of the moment of the sale, the whole process needs to be seen from the opposite end of the telescope – the customer. In fact, the whole business hinges on what the customer gets from you. So, design your business through the eyes of the customer.

A message to the marketing professionals

I have no intention of alienating or attacking our marketing professionals (managers, directors, consultants and academics) who all fall under the loose banner of 'doing marketing'.

From a distance one sometimes sees a slavish devotion to the discipline of marketing; what sometimes seems lacking is the passion and determination that is required, especially if you are trying to reach customers when you are a small growing business. What I yearn for is the focused enthusiasm, creativity and energy that can get decimated in larger organisations.

My tone may sometimes sound aggressive, but my intention is simply to focus on giving practical tips and advice that can be applied in the workplace.

For the marketing professionals, I wish to inspire you to do even better, more effective work by focusing and virtually obsessing on the customer experience.

This book is different from the rest

There are four reasons why this book is different:

> ■ This is not a text book filled with research-based, intellectually attractive theories: it is far more of a discussion and explanation of how to grow your business by understanding the customer experience.
>
> ■ This book is focused on methods and tools that are known to work in businesses like your own. It was created with the co-operation (and feedback) of businesses that have applied these tools to their own enterprises. The tools work.
>
> ■ The book is peppered with case studies and live examples of the issues that you are dealing with.
>
> ■ When you buy this book you get access to a web-based discussion forum where you can share your business issues with other like-minded businesspeople. Sign up now and join the Directors' Centre business community – express your views or ask for advice and support.
> http://www.yahoogroups.com/group/directorscentre.

Use the book

Use the book however you want. My only plea is that you do use the book as a lever to improve your business.

We have all flicked through various self-help volumes, chatted about the ideas in between the covers and then continued on our merry way, pretty much as before. For a book to impact on your business you need to do something different as a result of reading it. As you read the book, please think long and hard about how you can apply the various concepts to your business. How can you use this book to improve your business?

Your business will not change unless you act – action is at the heart of this book. I can only show you the tools to use; *you* must use them. Use the web-based discussion forum to let me and your fellow readers know what happens to you – share your success and your failures and what you have learned.

The mere fact that you feel driven to buy the book suggests that you want to make some changes. But buying the book is not enough. To get any kind of benefit, you need to work with your team to make the difference that makes the difference. This work will pay dividends.

Now is the time to go for it!

Robert Craven
rc@robert-craven.com
Bath, April 2002

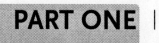

PART ONE

1: Why Marketing Sometimes Fails (especially for your business)

Marketing and marketers are under attack – their critics question the value that they add to a business. Put simply, traditional marketing behaves like the emperor's new clothes: the believers point and marvel at how wonderful it is. At the same time many feel that they invest a lot of time and money in marketing without getting the promised returns.

- Put your customer first.
- In a world where everything is increasingly the same, you must try to be different – otherwise, why should people bother to buy from you?
- Five reasons why marketing fails.
- Test your marketing effectiveness.

Opinion

It *seems* to be upside-down thinking to put your customers' interests ahead of your own – maybe that is why so many businesses are so totally unremarkable, so unmemorable and ultimately unsuccessful.

By all means go for the one-off quick sale, be obsessed with your profit – but the customer may not return. Focus on the needs of the client and you may not win that one-off profit, but you will profit in the long-run.

One-liner

If you're going to fall in love try not to fall in love with your product. Rather, try falling in love with the customer, because then you will do all you can in your power to keep them happy, and they'll appreciate it in the long run.

Opinion

While so many things (TV, films, clothes, cars) seem to be getting better, they are also getting increasingly alike: similar companies, employing similar people, with similar educational backgrounds, working in similar jobs, coming up with similar ideas, producing similar things, with similar prices and similar quality. It is no wonder that everything seems the same.

Blandness and sameness seem to have become the trademark of our time and yet it takes so little extra effort to make a product or service genuinely personalised or individualised.

For example, there are plenty of privately owned burger bars in our towns and yet most seem to insist on giving truly mediocre and artificial service – the bar that really does care about customers and the food that is being produced, stands out from the rest.

So what?

Often companies wonder why they are not busier or more profitable. In this world where your competitors make a similar product (or service) at a similar price, is it any wonder that you don't get more customers? Why should customers bother to buy from you when it is just as easy (or, worse still, easier) to buy from your competitors?

For example, there are plenty of places that would sell me a second-hand car for my son to learn to drive. Major Motors in Wiltshire go out of their way to find out what sort of car you are looking for and why and when you might be buying. Paul, the MD there, knows every one of his past and present customers and gives them his private home phone number; he literally does everything he can to find you the car that you want. Even if it means foregoing a profit, this time, so that a customer will return or recommend his business to someone else.

Fact?

To succeed, we must stop being so goddamn normal. In a winner-takes-all world, normal equals nothing.

Five reasons why marketing fails (especially for your business)

We can fire bullets at the 'marketing establishment' until the cows come home. But that is neither constructive nor helpful. There are, however, some basic reasons why marketing appears to be failing in many businesses. Some typical comments are:

1. 'It is difficult to equate marketing spend with outputs.'
2. 'You never know when or if marketing has worked, or whether it actually helps.'
3. 'Marketers seem to be abstract, remote and conceptual.'
4. 'Marketers often do not understand the complexity or sophistication of the product that they are trying to sell.'
5. 'Marketers often appear to be "above" walking around the shop floor, where the real work in the business takes place!'

ACTION POINT: Quick marketing audit

Why and how do you think your marketing effort is disappointing? What score out of ten would you give your marketing effort (where ten is a brilliant score and zero is atrocious)?

Your score out of ten for your marketing: _____

List three recent occasions where you feel that your marketing could have been better:

1 _____

2 _____

3 _____

List five reasons for this poor performance:

1 _____

2 _____

3 _____

4 _____

5 _____

List five ways you could improve your marketing performance:

1 _____

2 _____

3 _____

4 _____

5 _____

If you could improve your marketing performance, list five ways that your business would benefit:

1 _____

2 _____

3 _____

4 _____

5 _____

Simply having a knowledge of the issues that you have listed above will not help your business very much. To an outsider it may even sound as if you are simply whingeing and complaining. A specific type of action is required.

So, let me be specific about the main reasons why marketing activities may fail in your business. The list is simple.

Lack of commitment

If you don't really believe in your product, or if you are not consistent and regular in the ways that you promote it, then the odds are that you will not succeed. Your plans must ensure that you have committed the appropriate resources and effort to do what it takes to make your product work.

Lack of a clear benefit

It never hurts to state the obvious: you must sell something that people want. So you have to get close to your customer (or potential customer) and find out what they really want, and examine what it is that you have to offer. Please don't just make the things that you find easy or fun to make. Customers do not care about how much fun you've had. They will be asking the WIIFM question, 'What's In It For Me?'

Poor positioning

If you look exactly the same as your competitors and you offer the same benefits at the same price, then why should customers bother to come to you? You need clarity about what it is that you offer and why customers should come to you. This, in turn, will inform you as to how to promote and present yourself effectively.

KISS

Keep It Simple, Stupid! We all seem to have an ability to complicate things without realising that simplicity, clarity and focus will bring us the profits we seek.

Paralysis by analysis combined with dull thinking

This is normally brought on by attending too many inappropriate marketing courses and reading too many textbooks aimed at professional marketing departments of large companies (where they are unlikely to be as flexible – or feel the need to change – as in a smaller business)!

Most of the problems for the growing business are those that can be called 'transactional' – in other words, things like making customer contacts, getting orders, meeting the right people. Despite this fact, most business advice either refuses to deal with delivering the practical hands-on support required or is stuck in its big-business roots, which tend to be preoccupied with administrative issues.

ACTION POINT: Test your marketing effectiveness

Score yourself in the following test. Be honest – and always recall specific examples of actions carried out, rather than imagine 'hoped-for' situations. Focus on something real, or even better, get someone else to score your business (a customer or a supplier would be in an ideal position to score you and give you some fascinating feedback at the same time).

Mark a percentage score for each of the following questions:

---

1. We are totally committed to our marketing and sales plans (if we have them in the first place!).

0% – 10 – 20 – 30 – 40 – 50 – 60 – 70 – 80 – 90 – 100%
In Your dreams   On a good day   Got It!

2. Customers know exactly what they get if they come to us.

0% – 10 – 20 – 30 – 40 – 50 – 60 – 70 – 80 – 90 – 100%
In Your dreams   On a good day   Got It!

3. Customers know why we are different from the rest.

0% – 10 – 20 – 30 – 40 – 50 – 60 – 70 – 80 – 90 – 100%
In Your dreams   On a good day   Got It!

4. We make everything simple and easy to understand for our customers and for ourselves.

0% – 10 – 20 – 30 – 40 – 50 – 60 – 70 – 80 – 90 – 100%
In Your dreams   On a good day   Got It!

5. Decision-making is easy because we are clear about what we are trying to do.

0% – 10 – 20 – 30 – 40 – 50 – 60 – 70 – 80 – 90 – 100%
In Your dreams   On a good day   Got It!

Come back to this test once you have learned more about seeing things through the customers' eyes – the difference will be a revelation to you.

How did you score? I have yet to come across a business that, in its heart of hearts, couldn't find a way to improve in most areas. Most people get that familiar comment that I used to get in my school reports: 'Could do better'.

A few thoughts:

- Can you think of any specific area where you could have done better?
- Can you think of anything that you could do this week, or even today, that could improve any of your scores?
- What's holding you back from getting on with these actions?

Consider

A growing number of people feel that marketing (as it is commonly presented) is failing to deliver. Are you part of that number? Do you come out of marketing seminars and resent the intellectually fascinating but unearthed, disconnected way that the subject relates to real actions and results? Is this you?

So what?

Most marketing books claim that a new way of looking at things, a 'new paradigm', is required; what is really needed is a way of finding and satisfying customers that is *simple yet effective*!

Problems with sales and marketing

When you listen to the comments that people make when talking about marketing, you can hear that it is *help* that they are actually seeking. The following are pretty standard comments:

- **What they say**: 'Our pricing is easily matched/bettered by our competitors, who seem to surpass and outflank us.'
- **What they mean**: 'We're a pretty run-of-the-mill, mediocre organisation and our competition is at least as good as we are. To be quite frank, sometimes I am pretty surprised that we do any business at all!'

- **What they say**: 'Advertising is getting more expensive and less effective; too much time and money is spent on sales promotion and we don't know how effective it is.'
- **What they mean**: 'We still do the same ads but we really haven't got a clue why we do it any more – isn't doing the same thing and expecting a different result simply a definition of insanity?'

- **What they say**: 'Sales-force costs are rising.'
- **What they mean**: 'I wonder why we can't sell our product as easily as in the past – personally I blame the sales force.'

- **What they say**: 'Our so-called "innovative" projects often don't look much different from those of our competitors.'
- **What they mean**: 'When it comes to doing things differently, we are a pretty uninspired bunch of people.'

- **What they say**: 'A lot is being given away.'
- **What they mean**: 'In a desperate effort to sell more, we thought that we could improve margins by giving our stuff away for free, and now the punters don't see why they should pay the premium prices that we have to charge to recoup our losses from giving our product away in the first place.'

- **What they say**: 'We don't have a clear view of the future.'
- **What they mean**: 'Don't tell anyone but I think that we've lost the plot.'

It is only the last comment that concedes *our* own role in sorting out *our* business – most businesses look everywhere except to themselves to see how they can run a better concern. Adopting the principles in this book will make your business more effective, more efficient and more profitable.

Connect

As the British Telecom adverts say, 'It's good to talk.' Your customers should be treated like friends – trusted and trusting friends. Try treating them as such.

Randomly select, say, ten names from your customer database. Commit to contacting them all in the next week. However, when you contact them this time, try doing it as if you actually care: be more compassionate or loyal then you usually are. Use a more personal means of communicating – a personal phone call or a handwritten letter or postcard will always be more powerful than a faceless email. See if you don't notice the difference when you start making more effort to communicate with your clients. You don't have to phone up to sell: you can phone for a chat ('I was just thinking about you . . .' or 'I just realised that it's simply ages since we . . .')

Summary

Think 'customers' all the time – look at your business through their eyes. Try to make it as easy as possible for people to do business with you. Customers are not academic abstractions: they are real people with real needs and unless you can relate to them and their needs then you will not do very well in business.

2: The Customer Experience: What People Really Buy

The 'customer experience' is what happens to the customer when they buy, use, repair, replace or think about using your product or service. If you can understand what they experience (what they think, feel, believe and say about the experience) then you can design your offering to improve things for the customer so that they will want to buy more from you.

- You must figure out the most powerful benefit or advantage that your product offers so that it will be totally irrational for a potential customer to buy from someone else.
- Find what it is that your customers think they are buying.

Question
Why do people buy from you instead of from your competitors?

Answer
There are four possible answers:

1. You know exactly what unique set of advantages you offer your clients, and you set out to capitalise on these advantages.
2. You offer a unique set of advantages, but you've never really identified them yourself.
3. You offer the client no unique set of advantages and you're just lucky to be still trading.
4. You are about to go out of business because you are virtually giving the stuff away!

Fact
Keith Morton, managing director of Wines2You, recently commented that the most important thing he took away from a work-

shop session he attended was the following fact: the only products that succeed are those that offer a benefit to consumers that is greater than the cost (to them).

So what?
Do you offer a benefit to your customers/consumers that is greater than the cost to them?

I know that this is obvious, but often we are in the *business* of (re-)stating the obvious. If you are not offering a benefit greater than the cost to the customer then it is you who will lose in every sense.

One-liner
You must figure out the most powerful benefit or advantage that your product offers, so that it will be totally irrational for a potential customer to buy from someone else.

Fact
People normally buy 'benefits' and not 'features'.

So what?
The trouble is, often when we run our own business we get so preoccupied with the features that we have given the product that we forget why the customer might wish to buy it in the first place!

The difference between 'features' and 'benefits'

Typically, the feature is an attribute, a characteristic; the benefit is why the consumer wants it:

Feature	Benefit
128k RAM	Faster performance
Large type	Ease of reading
Digital recording	Hiss-free sound
Ergonomic design	No backache
Rolls-Royce logo	Increased self-esteem

I am currently thinking of buying a new car. As I consider what I want, I list the following as my key criteria:

- safety
- comfortable seat
- space for kids and luggage
- cheap to run

It is not too difficult to translate these benefits into features. But please remember that it is the benefit and not the feature that will sell me the car.

For example:

Feature	Benefit
Twin airbags, side-impact bars	Safety
Computer-controlled multiposition driver seat	Comfortable driving position for me and my partner
Larger-than-average back seat	Space for kids
6 cubic metres of boot	Space for luggage
43 m.p.g. at a constant 56 m.p.h.	Cheap to run

Now, analyse your products and services in this way – are the benefits that you are offering your customers clear enough?

ACTION POINT: Matching benefits to features

First, list your features. Second, list the relevant benefit next to each feature – if you have difficulty describing a benefit, just add the words 'which means that' after the feature (and before the benefit) to help you to connect the two.

For example, sleek design (feature), 'which means that' it looks good in your living room (benefit).

Feature	Benefit

Even better, seven questions to ask your customers

Visit some of your customers, or talk to them at your premises or when you are next in phone contact. Ask them some of the following questions:

- 'What do you buy our product to do?'
- 'How do you use our product?'
- 'How does our product/service help you?'
- 'What are the features of our product/service that you really value?'
- 'How do these features help you?'
- 'What really irritates you about our product/service?'
- 'What would you do if you were us to get more sales from you?'

You will need to refine these questions to suit your business. Below is a transcript from one of these mini-surveys, carried out by Grisholm Office Supplies, who were focusing on their sales of photocopiers.

- **Question**: 'How do you use the photocopiers that you buy from us?' ('What do you buy our product to do?')
  Reply: 'We put them into our smaller departments to do all the day-to-day small-quantity photocopy needs. Big runs we send to our print department.'

- **Question**: 'What are the main things you use our machines for?' ('How do you use our product?')
  Reply: 'Just about all the work is straight one-to-one copies, A4 to A4 paper. All the fancy stuff like blowing up or reduction is done at the print department.'

- **Question**: 'How does the way that we work actually help you to do a better job? ('How does our product/service help you?')
  Reply: 'What we like is that it is a no-nonsense service – we phone you, tell you what we want and you deliver it and install it within 48 hours.'

- **Question**: 'What do you like about the way that we do business – what aspects of our systems and processes do you find good?' ('What are the features of our product/service that you really value?')

Reply: 'Being able to order by email or on the web is excellent. The fact that you always leave ten reams of paper with the machine is great, especially if we are putting a machine into a department that has never had one before. And free servicing for the first six months is quite neat.'

■ **Question**: 'So, can you explain how these features help you?' ('How do these features help you?')

Reply: 'The web thing is incredibly convenient, and easy to use. The paper means that we don't have to panic about sorting paper supplies for a while, which, believe it or not, takes a whole lot of pressure off us. We are driven by our systems and codes you know! And the servicing bit . . . well it is just reassuring to know that, once a machine is installed, it will be looked after and again we can set up a proper service agreement in our own time (more purchase orders and requisition forms!).'

■ **Question**: 'What really irritates you about our service?'

Reply: 'When I do phone up, I always seem to speak to a different person – what's going on there? Can't you keep the staff? Oh, and what about a paper catalogue? The web thing is great but I can hardly show it to the finance department. We like something to have in our hands that we can pass around. Our computer system is so depressingly slow that it is a wonder that we see a whole web page sometimes. And another thing: half the time your phones are switched to answerphone – is there no one there to answer the phones? And sometimes our people don't really understand how the machines work – well, not properly. It always ends up being a bit of guesswork, the blind leading the blind, so to speak.'

■ **Question**: 'What would you do if you were us to get more sales from you?'

Reply: 'One, get your act together – your business comes across as a bit of a shambles sometimes. Two, contact us with a newsletter or something. It always seems to be us contacting you. Three, a discount for loyal service wouldn't go amiss. Four, can't we sort one big service contract for all the machines rather than an agreement for each machine? Five, how about spending a bit more time training up our people how to use the machines?'

As a result of this and similar feedback, Grisholm did the following:

- **account manager** appointed for each customer
- **training sessions** arranged at each client's place of business
- **phone system** rationalised so that there is always a person answering the phone (by using an external phone-answering service)
- a brief **'special offers' flyer** sent out every month
- quarterly **review sessions** with each client arranged to ensure continuity and contact
- an annual Grisholm **'open day'** held for existing and potential and past customers
- prices increased but all existing clients simultaneously offered **discounts**
- customers shown the **full range of facilities** on each machine and, if they were not required, then a lower specification (i.e. cheaper) machine would be recommended

Summary

Go out and find what it is that your customers think they are buying. Do not make any assumptions – hear it from the proverbial 'horse's mouth'. Ask questions, and, when you think that you have asked enough questions, ask some more!

3: The Difference Between 'Wants' and 'Needs'

Key to the thought processes in this book is also the difference between 'wants' and 'needs'.

- ■ Understand what people want.
- ■ Effectively communicate the benefits (of buying from you) to the consumer/customer.

There is a difference between what I actually need and what I think that I want.

> **For example:** To be more attractive, I think I want a Gucci watch (a want); I actually *need* to smarten myself up.
>
> **For example:** To run a better business, I think I want a better website; I actually *need* to understand what it is that people really buy from me.
>
> **For example**: I think I want to drink more alcohol; I actually *need* to go to bed and think about what I have been saying.

If we can understand the difference between consumers' wants and needs then we can start to see where we, as their suppliers, fit in! We can start to see how we can talk directly to the consumer's psyche!

Most of us have what we need: food, shelter, warmth and clothing. As a result, most marketers are no longer concerned with dealing with needs. What we are actually focusing on is the consumer's wants and desires.

So a standard list of wants and desires might include some of the following:

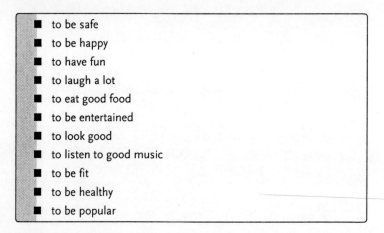

- to be safe
- to be happy
- to have fun
- to laugh a lot
- to eat good food
- to be entertained
- to look good
- to listen to good music
- to be fit
- to be healthy
- to be popular

A cynic would say that people buy a product for one of two reasons:

- to make them happier, or
- to make them more profitable

And even Shakespeare said, 'No profit grows where is no pleasure ta'en.'

So what?

Products and services sell for many times their manufactured cost. And the reason that people will pay this premium is because of a belief that the product will deliver the benefit. And the 'value' of the benefit will exceed the price paid.

Give me an example

Over the last ten years I have done a lot of work with business support agencies. Typically, their clients come to them because of what they think they need (i.e. a want). What the client actually needs is normally very different.

The list of wants is endless, but the Top 10 looks as follows:

1. Free money or a grant
2. To be rid of the bank manager and/or my debts
3. Better cash flow
4. A website
5. Better brand awareness
6. An advertising campaign
7. More customers
8. More sales
9. Better customers
10. A new product

The list of what clients actually need looks somewhat different:

1. A keen understanding of how the customer actually experiences the business (a.k.a. **marketing**)
2. An understanding of why the customer goes to the business and what makes the organisation different from the rest (a.k.a. **marketing strategy**)
3. A clarity about where the business wants to be in three years' time, so where it needs to be in a year's time, so what it needs to do now – planning while being aware of the business environment (a.k.a. **strategy**)
4. The ability to recruit, train, motivate and retain a brilliant team (a.k.a. **people**)
5. The financial resources, management skills, processes and systems (a.k.a. **finances**)
6. The discipline to measure, monitor and evaluate all business processes (a.k.a. **processes**)

The skill of the experienced adviser is to get the client to recognise what they really need.

Questions for your business

- What is it that potential customers say they want when they visit you?
- What is it that they actually need?

> ■ How do you persuade them of what they need? Or do you let them buy what they want? (Don't forget: you know how annoying it is when you go into a shop to buy Product A and they tell you that what you really need is Product Z!)

Linking benefits and desires to products (or brands)

Returning to some of the examples that were used earlier, you can see how the products below have benefits that appeal directly to the wants and desires as outlined above. Below, I have listed a few brands and the benefit (often a single word) that is associated with them. I have deliberately chosen brand names that you will recognise, but do remember that these are being used *as examples* to help you to take the idea and to translate it into your business).

Some brands and the associated benefit:

> ■ Volvo cars (safety)
> ■ Gap clothing (look good)
> ■ delicatessen food (good food)
> ■ Billy Connolly video (laughter)

What does this mean for you

Gap and Volvo are companies that have spent years nurturing their brands and brand values – but your business can learn from the big boys. Take the method of thinking explained above and start to apply it to your business.

Key questions

> ■ What word do you want people to associate with your business?
> ■ If there isn't *one* word that springs to mind, then what are the *words*? Are the different words relatively consistent or do they seem to have little in common? So, does your business transmit a consistent message?
> ■ Using a metaphor for your business, what animal would you want people to think of in association with your organisation?

- What word springs to mind when people think of your business? (Ask them.)
- What animal springs to mind when people think of your business? (Ask them.)
- How can you get nearer to the desired state? What do you need to do? How could you do it?

A key issue for your business

At the heart of your business you must be able to:

- understand what people want, and
- effectively communicate the benefits (of buying from you) to the consumer/customer

You will not be successful if you do not understand these key elements of 'being a customer'. And to be really successful you need to go beyond these maxims!

Questions of your business

- What are the features of one of your products?
- What is the benefit that the customer buys?
- Does all your publicity material focus on benefits to customers (good!) or features that you've put into the product (usually wrong!)?

Law 14 of The Immutable Laws of Customer-Focused Marketing*

Customers buy benefits and proofs – show them the advantages and features but make sure the benefits and proofs address their problem.

There is real power to be gained from seeing things through the customer's eyes. As the saying goes, 'If you want to understand a Red Indian, spend a day walking in his/her moccasins.' Likewise, if you can see your business from the customer's point of view, then

*These laws are dealt with in full in Part Three of the book.

you will get real insight into what does and what does not work in your business. And you will see where you can make relatively small improvements that can have a big impact on your effectiveness.

When looking through the customer's eyes always think 'What's in it for me?' (WIIFM). As producers or makers or providers of a service, we find it easy to get preoccupied with what is put into the product (the features). Customers are much more interested in what is in it for *them* (they focus on benefits); and how well you can demonstrate these benefits (the proofs) will determine the potential customer's response.

In workshops we sometimes refer to the 'P-FAB-P' Law. By 'P-FAB-P' we refer to **Problem**, **Features**, **Advantages**, **Benefits** and **Proofs**. To sell effectively you need to:

- identify the **Problem**
- understand that **Features** tend to be what you focus on
- show the **Advantages** of your offering . . .
- . . . which make clear **Benefits** of your solution
- and people will buy from you if you can show them **Proofs** that your system will work for them!

For example:

- I get bad backache when sitting in front of my computer (the **Problem**).
- The Aeon Chair is made by a unique method using unique materials (I won't bore you with the details) (the **Features**).
- It is the only seat with the number of different seat positions and special materials available on the market (the **Advantages**).
- The chair will make sitting in front of my computer a backache-free pleasure so that I can be more productive, with no lost hours and no expensive osteopath bills, and the seat will look dead modern in my office (the **Benefits**).
- I know people who swear by these chairs; I have read testimonials from the good and the great who claim that they could not live without the chair (the **Proof**).

One-liner

Every sales pitch should use the phrase 'which means that ...' to ensure that you are explaining how your product will solve your customer's problem.

Summary

Do not confuse wants with needs (and do not confuse features with benefits). Think, live and breathe the 'customer'. People buy benefits, not features – and they want to see the proof that there are benefits available for them. If you want to make the customer feel important then you must focus on demonstrating your benefits through the use of proofs.

4: Madame Praline and her Customer Experience

Monty Python's 'Dead Parrot' sketch personifies bad service. The shopkeeper is not interested in the customer. In fact it seemed as if the shopkeeper went out of his way to be as rude and obnoxious as possible.

■ Do your customers ever get a 'dead parrot' experience when they visit your business? (Never, ever? Occasionally?)

To my absolute disbelief, I recently experienced a remarkable sense of *déjà vu* as a shopkeeper re-enacted Monty Python's 'Dead Parrot' sketch. What was really farcical about the situation that I was watching was that the shopkeeper was totally unaware that he was replicating a situation that was a comic (almost tragic) event. As I am sure you recall, the original sketch featured John Cleese as an irate customer trying to complain to the pet-shop owner about his dead parrot. For the purpose of the following 'transcript' I have named the lady watch buyer Madame Praline, after John Cleese's frustrated Mr Praline and his dead parrot.

My spooky re-enactment took place in Paris – I will translate what I witnessed. My French is not perfect but the whole scenario did have a Pythonesque feel.

MADAME PRALINE: Hello. I wish to make a complaint.

(The owner has his back to her and does not respond.)

MADAME PRALINE: I said I wish to make a complaint! I wish to complain about this watch that I purchased not three weeks ago.

OWNER: Oh yes, the Stafford 210. What's, er . . . W-what's wrong with it?

MADAME PRALINE: I'll tell you what's wrong with it. It's broken. That's what's wrong with it.

OWNER: No, no, its not broken. We don't sell broken watches.

MADAME PRALINE: Look, Monsieur, I know a broken watch when I see one, and I'm looking at one right now.

OWNER: No, no, it's not broken, but I expect you don't know how to work it – it is in hibernation mode.

MADAME PRALINE: Hibernation mode?

OWNER: Y-yeah, hibernation mode. Remarkable watch the Stafford 210, isn't it, eh? Beautiful strap!

MADAME PRALINE: The strap doesn't enter into it. It's broken!

OWNER: Nonononono, no, no! It's in hibernation mode!

MADAME PRALINE: All right then, if it's hibernating, let's wake it up!

(She shakes the watch really hard)

OWNER: There, the hand moved!

MADAME PRALINE: No, it didn't, this is a broken watch – you sold me a dead watch and I want a new one. I have tried a new battery twice and I have tried pressing all buttons as suggested in the instructions, and basically this watch does not work.

(She tosses it up in the air and watches it plummet to the floor. Longish pause.)

OWNER: Now that's what I call a broken watch.

(Madame Praline walks out of the shop!)

Madame Praline is typical of many so-called 'empowered' customers. She has paid her money and yet she knows that she has been cheated. All she wanted was what she thought she had paid for – a working watch. In fact, had there been an innocent error made by the shopkeeper then the complaint might not have got out of hand. It is the shopkeeper's insistence that there is nothing the matter with the watch that drives Madame Praline so mad.

What can we learn from Madame Praline?

How often have *you* felt like Madame Praline? You get driven to distraction by some small-minded, officious shopkeeper or so-called customer-service assistant who refuses to see things the way that you do.

Was Madame Praline justified in becoming so cross? I think so. What could the shop owner have done? Was he programmed to wind up poor Madame Praline?

The shop owner never intended to be honest with Madame Praline. In the original 'Dead Parrot' sketch I recall that the parrot is nailed to the perch – the shop owner claims that this is to ensure that the parrot doesn't escape. 'Well, of *course* it was nailed there!' he says. 'If I hadn't nailed that bird down, it would have nuzzled up to those bars, bent 'em apart with its little pecker, and *voom!*'

The Paris incident is so hilarious because it is so close to so many experiences that we all have had.

What could the owner have done to turn Madame Praline around? Do you think that Madame Praline was always going to be unsatisfied?

Hmm ... something to think about
Do your customers ever get a 'dead parrot' experience when they visit your business? (Never, ever? Occasionally?)

Hmm ... something to keep you awake at night

- Do any of your competitors give their customers a 'dead parrot' experience? (So what?)
- Do you get many Mr/Madame Pralines as customers? (What do you do with them? What do they say about you? Could you deal with them in a better way?)
- What can you do to make sure that you don't get Madame Pralines as customers?
- More importantly, what can you do to make sure that your business doesn't have any people who behave like that shop owner?

Summary

Look carefully at your own business. Get to understand what it feels like to be a customer of yours. Be clear about what people want (and/or need) to buy when they visit you. Design your business around what you want your customers to experience.

How can you improve the way your customers feel about you right now? Do it. And do not forget the 'Dead Parrot' sketch – most of us have been on both sides of the counter at some time. Mediocrity is simply not good enough for you or for your customers. You can do so much better!

5: Is the Customer Really in Charge?

The modern business's secret, which is neither dirty nor little, is that the customer runs the new show! And the biggest lie today (as put out by marketing departments) is that 'the customer is in charge'. Another secret is not that customer service is bad; everybody knows that! The other secret is that it's harder to deliver good customer service than ever before. And customers are more demanding.

- If every company wants to delight its customers, then how come we don't spend most of our customer days delighted?
- What would happen if you did put your customers in charge?

The reason that big business was, and is still, so excited about the web is the belief that 'the customer is in charge'. What nonsense! Well, sometimes. Let's briefly use the example of Cisco to see what can happen. I know, they are not small (like you) but they still make an impressive case study. What can you learn from the following?

Case study: Look, no humans!

Cisco Systems get 90 per cent of their $20 billion of revenues straight off the web with no human intervention or interference. Those who do business with Cisco exclusively through the web report customer satisfaction scores that are way above those of Cisco's customers who do business via people.

Moral of the story

The Cisco, Dell and Amazon secrets are roughly the same: engage the customer! Put the customer in charge!

For example, Cisco powered up some innocent 'chat rooms' for customer engineers. The process has now evolved into full-scale, 'virtual', 'collaborative design' activities. Cisco estimates it harvests over $1 billion in 'free' consulting from customer engineers. As of the last quarter of 2000, some 45,000 customer problems per week were being solved on the web via customer collaboration. There was no Cisco intervention other than the construction and maintenance of the website.

Tom Peters, in *The Circle of Innovation*, describes this as the DIY nation and quotes the former Oracle president, Ray Lanet: 'Changes in business processes will emphasise self-service. Your costs as a business go down and ... perceived service ... goes up because customers are conducting it themselves.'

You can then couple this DIY concept with the strongest force on earth. And the strongest force on earth is *one's need to be in perceived control of one's universe*!

This goes some way to explain why Ann Busquet, an American Express executive, says that, in fact, this is not the 'Age of the Internet; it is: the Age of Customer Control'.

To be more accurate, Regis McKenna, Silicon Valley's marketing guru No. 1, calls it 'the Age of the Never Satisfied Customer'. 'The moral is,' say two Mercer Consulting execs, Adrian Slywotzky and David Morrison, 'that in an imperfect world of customer service, most customers prefer to cut to the chase and help themselves.'

Meanwhile, the Swedish business strategy gurus Kjell Nordstrom and Jonas Ridderstrale, in *Funky Business* state, 'The Web enables total transparency. People with access to relevant information are beginning to challenge any type of authority. The stupid, loyal and humble customer, employee, patient or citizen is dead.' On and on it goes. Dotcom crash notwithstanding, no assertion is too extreme.

So what?

It would appear that the consumer, at a retail or commercial level, is taking charge. This is the power of the Internet and its associated technologies.

The big issue?
Is your strategy literally centred on customer/client empowerment and self-determination? (And, most notably for the larger business, this would mean letting go of traditional sources of power.)

The emperor's new clothes?

The so-called new economy and most new business have been built around a specific promise. This promise is that the 'customer is in charge'. The reality is that customer service has reached the pits. Call centres in the depths of the countryside leave us hanging on while we listen to more piped music.

As customers, we feel betrayed. It seems remarkable that an entire business philosophy, a mantra chanted across the modern world, is so obviously without substance. Many banks, universities, shops, restaurants, builders' merchants and software companies patently fail to deliver. The customer is not king. The customer is left waiting to be heard (again!).

To reflect on what has happened, one of the promises of the new-economy evangelists was that the customer would finally be in charge. We weren't supposed to need to call the customer-care department because everything would be right first time! But, if we did need to call the company for help, then (so the theory went) there would be a calm and understanding person waiting to take your call, a person who would be able to solve your problem instantly by having the right, relevant information at hand. And the result would be the delighted customer.

The reality is somewhat different. How often does the call centre tell you, 'We are experiencing higher than usual call volumes' or 'All our customer service operatives are currently busy' or 'You are in a queue'? This first statement is almost always followed by the second (incongruous) comment, 'We value your call.'

If they value my call then why do I always have to wait? If they are experiencing higher than usual call volumes then why don't we (the customers) experience higher than average staffing levels?

Basically, the new economy was meant to make service better, quicker and more effective for customers. At the same time it was meant to make it easier and cheaper for the companies. So much for the theory.

The gurus and evangelists have taken us for a journey (or do I mean they've taken us for a ride?) starting with 'meeting customer expectations', then moving on to exceeding 'customer expectations', through to 'delighting customers' and on to 'customer intimacy' and now to 'customer ecstasy'. So what's next, customer orgasm?

Finally the companies are starting to wake up to the fact that the customer is actually very angry with them. Customer-service ratings are a nonsense – the average score is always 'above average'.

ACTION POINT: Customer-view league table of competitors

Draw up some lists based on the following:

- Create a league table of your key competitors. Using a 'customer view', position each business in terms of how well they put the customer 'in control'.
- Ask yourself what things you could do tomorrow to improve your position in the 'customer-in-control league table'.
- List ten ways you can make your customers *feel* as if they are more in control.
- List ten ways actually *to put* your customers more in control.
- And list ten ways to communicate to customers how they *are* more in control when they buy from you.

Case study: Food for thought

Thai HiSi had been a popular Thai restaurant but had lost its edge as the owner, Joe, had been ill. On returning to the business Joe created a league table on the lines suggested above (names have been changed to 'protect the innocent').

First, he drew up his league table as suggested in the first point above:

Competitors	Customer in control?	League table position
The Posh Indian	No	5=
The Other Thai Restaurant	A bit	2=
The French Bistro	Yes	1
The Turkish Restaurant	A bit	2=
The Chinese Bar	A bit	2=
The Fine Eatery	No	5=

The exercise revealed to Joe that very few customers would 'feel in control'. On the big assumption that people want 'to be in control', then Joe set out to move himself off the bottom and up the league table.

On the second point – what things he could do tomorrow to improve his position in the 'customer-in-control league table' – Joe's answer was, 'Make the place friendlier, have more staff who were available and accessible, make the menu less daunting, inject some fun into the place, let the customer feel in control, focus on really fresh produce, let the customer see what's going on in the kitchen.'

What were his ten ways to make customers *feel* as if they are more in control? Joe's answer never made a full ten, but he did come up with eight! 'Let them take the order themselves; limit the choice; let the customers choose the actual ingredients and give them to the chef; let the customers watch their own food being cooked; let the customer bring their own wine; let customers choose where they are going to sit; stop formality and have lots of big tables where customers can sit with people they don't know; let the customer into the kitchen.'

Ten ways actually *to put* customers more in control? Here are some of the ten. Joe changed the restaurant to create a viewable kitchen; he put two tables in the kitchen so customers could actually sit in there; he gave customers preprinted pads on which to write their orders; he limited the range of dishes (making it easier for them to choose and also for Joe to guarantee a fresher meal); he let customers select ingredients for the stir-fries and hand them to the chef, who would use a big wok to cook each dish; he trained all staff to be extra-accessible.

As for the ten ways to communicate to customers how they are more in control? The main thing Joe did was to ensure that all the marketing materials and layout emphasised the unique aspects of the business: tables in the kitchen, choosing of customers' own food, taking customers' own orders.

The local clientele loved this new experience and transformed a mediocre restaurant into a huge success.

Summary

Clearly, most customers do not feel 'in charge'. You can use this to your advantage – think how easy it can become to stand out from the rest when you really *do* put the customer in charge! Customers have been told that they should be in charge and yet they rarely, if ever, feel as though they *are* in charge. So see what happens if you *do* put them in charge.

6: The New Context: 'When the World is Spinning Round'

How real is an Irish pub in Hampstead? Or a 'retro' car? We all hate to feel that we have been conned. And yet big businesses seem to be making a fortune by going out of their way to con us with contrivances and manipulations that are clearly false. The consumer then 'plays the game', pretending to know that the game is not real while desperately wanting to believe the illusion. This is something else that you can use to your advantage.

- Real relationships blow away the sizzle of institutional hype.
- Most consumers are more cash-rich and time-poor than ever before.
- X-O-X may be one formula for 'franchising' your idea (and making money) but the process of duplication stops 'your' business still being personal – it may destroy the very reason that you started the business.
- Do you want to be big and rich or smaller and sincere?

Real relationships blow away the sizzle of institutional hype. Customers know when they are being conned. You could argue that they get what they deserve, what they have asked for.

There are huge opportunities for the independent-minded business in this world of mediocrity, of insipid service and lack of attention to the detail that really matters.

In almost every market, the dominance of the 'big boys' is resented. In their search for reliability, conformity and profitability they almost always forget about the customer and the people who work at the business. Nine times out of ten, the local (and/or smaller) business may not be cheaper but can outperform in terms of attention to service, detail, product knowledge and customer understanding. So the idea of a 'Campaign for Real Businesses' is not so half-baked.

Large businesses cannot flex and respond and listen to the customer the way that a smaller business can. The energy and enthusiasm and excitement that a smaller business can generate (in staff and customers) can make the simplest shopping task quite pleasurable.

In a world where service levels seem to be collapsing (despite the growth in meaningless and empty service-level agreements and customer charters), the business that does really care and is really interested in doing great work can stand head and shoulders above the rest.

The question is whether you wish to rise to the challenge and how you actually make this happen 24 hours a day, seven days a week?

Money is no object

Most consumers are more cash-rich and time-poor than ever before. The average UK household is over twice as well off in real terms as it was in 1970, and over 50 per cent better off than in 1985 (*Director*, June 2001).

What seems to be happening, increasingly, is that there is a real desire for intangible, service-based things rather than just products. Consumers are tired of acquiring possessions and want more out of retail than just things.

Since most consumers can afford most material possessions (a TV, a video, a car) they are now turning towards one of two things. On the one hand they want things that are specifically different (i.e. branded) products; on the other hand they want an increased leisure quality. To verify this concept we need look no further than the popularity of Naomi Klein's *No Logo*, the business book with the powerful critique of the power of brands and the growing scepticism and dissatisfaction of consumers.

Success is a confusing thing for the growing business. You seek the popularity and profits that go with it; but, then again, your product loses its intimacy with the success; your customers cease to get the individual attention that you were once able to give to them.

A formula for success on a plate (or in a burger bun!)

One formula for success revolves around the 'X-O-X' Principle. With an Ordinary system it doesn't matter how *extraordinary* your people are: at the end of the day you will get Ordinary results as the mediocrity of the system will inevitably dominate.

What you really want to achieve is an 'X-O-X' system. An eXtraordinary system with Ordinary people will create eXtraordinary results. The 'X-O-X' system wins usually. This is what fast-food stores do – they put in place brilliant systems so that pretty ordinary folk can deliver extraordinary results.

The logical extension of this argument is as follows. If you wish to grow your business, you should create an 'X-O-X' system. If you get the system right and it can be run with the lowest common denominator in terms of employee skills then it can be replicated. In other words, you can clone your model, replicate it, as many times as you wish. This is what most franchise systems are based on.

All the major franchises (burgers, car parts, ties, etc.) apply the 'X-O-X' principle – burger bars consistently deliver the same quality throughout the world, served up by youngsters who have been trained to give a standard (and carefully researched) response to the situations they are presented with – the 'standard' way of greeting customers, or cooking fries, or mopping the floor. Every part of the system has been scrutinised and the 'best possible' way needs to be applied by the employee. So those Ordinary people using an eXtraordinary system have produced an eXtraordinary result.

The flaws in this argument are several. For a start, this way of thinking requires you to take as much skill out of the job as possible, so that you are not dependent on the qualifications and skills in your people – so the model will not be effective for 'brain work'.

Secondly, it predetermines that you are more interested in dollars than offering a genuine service. So, while this thinking may create a money machine, unfortunately most machines do not have hearts or souls!

And what has this to do with the customer?

The franchise system is a very effective business model. It delivers to a quality and it delivers a consistent product. It is also a very safe way to go into business. Buying into a tried and tested formula is more likely to succeed than making it up as you go along. At the heart of my argument is the customer. Most franchise systems assume that the customer has standard wants and needs – the system rarely caters for individual needs, attention to detail and the relationship. Franchises offer a 'machine' that works most of the time.

The success of the franchise offers real opportunities for other businesses. If you can take on board some of the franchise's good points (reliability, consistency) and add a personal touch, then maybe you will find a formula that can deliver what you want to deliver. Remember that most growing businesses fail because they are not prepared to take on all the 'business' stuff that they were trying to get away from: bureaucracy, systems, processes. Ironically, your success depends on the very things that so many small businesses try to escape from when they set up. The franchise simply recognises the need for a structured and methodical approach to 'delighting the customer' (even if it isn't using your definition of that phrase).

Time to reflect

If you hit upon a winning business formula, you have to make important choices. Should you expand, open another branch, franchise, license or what?

After all, if you've figured out a winning strategy, it seems only rational to cash in by letting the market have what it wants: more of you! Let's play the devil's advocate for a moment. As long as you're giving the market what it wants, what's the problem? If *some* is good, isn't *more* better?

However, the moment you start to take your special, authentic, limited-edition product and leverage it, make it widely available, the very people who loved it (also known as the 'early adopters' in marketing circles) will inevitably rebel.

'Starbucks isn't what it used to be,' they tell you. The early fans who made you successful in the first place turn on their heels when they smell that you're not authentic any more. 'Before ubiquity, or widespread popularity, when it seemed as if the product (or its creator) wasn't in it just for the money, somehow that felt more real, more wonderful, more authentic,' they say.

Where is all this heading?

Enter the demon (or deity, depending on your point of view) called marketing. Brands, logos, salesmanship, positioning and focus groups have become associated with corporate greed. It seems to be part of a game where 'they' are trying to win something over on 'us' (the consumer/customer). This mistrust of marketing comes from people's desire to have something real – and to get it from someone who isn't trying quite so hard to sell it.

So what?

So, the million-dollar question is 'Are we ever authentic?'

A burger chain or an amusement park clearly doesn't provide an authentic experience. It is a manufactured, designed, manipulated, processed experience aimed at maximising profit. (Who cares?)

The source of the debate is that, to us as consumers, almost everything we experience has this lack of authenticity and sincerity. We have been conned into these superficial relationships, yet we remember and relish human contact.

For instance, your local delicatessen gives you a better service (in most senses) than your supermarket. An independently owned and run pub or bar can give you a better, more personal service than one owned by a large chain. (Not always, but usually!)

Is this simply half-baked, tree-hugging veggie rubbish?

No. Put simply, the great advantage that the smaller or independent business has is its ability to create something relatively genuine and sincere – something that the people who run the enterprise actually believe in. When you discover that Irish bars or gay bars are simply part of a multinational drinks corporation that specialises in themed entertainment you realise that the whole experience is fake, shallow and insincere. You may have enjoyed the event, but you have been conned. (Again, who cares? you may argue!)

We might adore fresh goats' cheese made in tiny batches and bought on a farm in France. However, is it any different from the output from huge vats of goats' cheese produced by Kraft somewhere in the West and delivered weekly to your local supermarket? What if you couldn't tell them apart in a taste test? Which would taste better? (Again, who cares?)

Why does the intention of the creator of a product have so much influence on our perception of the product, and hence how we as consumers value the product/experience?

For the bigger business, the issue is how to reinstil the idea of adventure. Smaller businesses are already halfway there – closer to the customer, closer to the products and closer to staff; the growing business really is in a position genuinely to delight its customers!

It is the smaller, more nimble, more flexible business that can offer customers an authentic experience – the larger businesses can only pretend. And in a world where customers seem to get more and more disillusioned with the mass product, the producer of the authentic product or service can find opportunities (where they will be able to beat the big boys).

Paradoxes abound

The paradox is this. Markets talk. Word spreads. When something is great, we all want it. And if it is your product or service that they all want, then isn't that a great feeling!

As consumers, we often want produce to be local and reasonably priced. And we want reliability. We want it to be just as good each and every time we experience it.

At Hartley's Restaurant, a two-year-old West Country bistro, there was very little order or structure in the way that they ran things. They had to start becoming more and more formal (in their systems and the way that they did things) to guarantee that every quiche and every pie looked and tasted just as good as the previous ones. After all, to be inconsistent might upset customers.

But the very process of guaranteeing a specific quality meant that they were taking out the 'interesting', home-grown, amateur feel, and possibly replacing it with a monotonous consistency. Gone are the different individual cooking styles of different members of staff as they strive to deliver the 'house style'!

The conundrum

On the one hand, if something is going to be authentic, it needs to be rare and special and live. On the other, what is the difference between the authentic and the manufactured?

If you're lucky enough to create something authentic, you have real choices. You need to decide how important it is to be real, how much of yourself you have tied up in the authentic experience that you've created. Most of all, you need to decide what you'd like to do all day.

Some of us can be happy taking today's flavour and selling it like crazy. Often, for the smaller business the owner-manager is not prepared to sacrifice his or her belief in the way that he or she 'does' the product/service to make a few pounds. This self-limiting belief stops many owner-managers from going on to make their fortune. (And who are we to judge if that is right or wrong?)

Case study: Back to basics

Amanda Robson's Communication Company focused on helping chief executives and senior managers to make better presentations. Amanda's successful business model grew beyond her wildest dreams. Within 3 years she was employing 75 staff and 60 associates to help assist people with their presentation skills.

Amanda's original objective was to help, and to help through making her clients become better communicators. She loved the intimacy and intensity of the one-to-one relationships that she had with her clients. Because of her insistence that all relationships with clients should follow her strict and intense guidelines, the business grew and grew and grew.

However, running the business with no one-to-one work with clients (for herself) finally drove Amanda Robson mad. The business's success also sowed the seeds of its own destruction. Amanda woke up one day and realised that the business had become a Frankenstein's monster, albeit a profitable one. It was time to get back to what really excited her.

She made several brave decisions. She sold the business database. She closed the company. She sold all of the business assets. She went on a six-month world tour. When she returned she started up again on her own but vowing to employ no more than one personal assistant. Back to her roots, and that is how she has kept it.

Do people who create something authentic but then sell out almost always end up unhappy?

Once you sell out, any new success you have isn't because you are authentic. You're in a new business now. Would you be happy with that?

Case study: Jamie loses the plot

Jamie Dimmock has been a mentoring client of mine for several years. Financially he has been hugely successful. He has taken his food-processing company to the NASDAQ financial market, and raised millions in finance for a business that has grown at over 100 per cent a year. The business is hugely profitable, and Dimmock, aged 32, could cash in his shares in the business for about $15 million.

And yet he came to me in 2002 and was so unhappy: 'I'm worth millions but I can't find a challenge that turns me on any more. And what have I really achieved? I need something to keep me driven, but what can I do next? I don't want to see any more of my family and now my wife is worried that I am not the obsessive, driven person that I used to be. Well, I'm sure that something will turn up.' Poor Jamie had lost the plot.

The very passion and obsessive behaviour that had created his empire had also meant that he had ignored many of his more basic needs (friends and family); the only way he knew to turn himself on was by creating ever bigger mountains to climb until he had lost his passion.

Before you pull the trigger and sell out and scale up, consider a few questions:

- Is it better to be big than to be (perceived as) real?
- Is spreading the word more important than being admired by a tiny coterie of truly devoted fans?
- Should financial rewards only come to those who make good stuff for the masses?
- Could you be happy practising your authentic task for the rest of your life?

If you do get big, you won't be practising authenticity for the rest of your life. When you sell out, you're making a trade-off. The big market wants reliability and conformity. The big market probably won't reward you for being authentic.

As Oscar Wilde says in *The Importance of Being Earnest*, 'In matters of grave importance, style, not sincerity, is the vital thing.'

'Sincerity's the main thing,' the movie mogul Samuel Goldwyn once confessed, 'and, once you learn to fake that, everything else is easy.'

I saw a performance by the comedian Billy Connolly. A heckler called out, 'Tell us a joke, you rich ugly bastard.' Connolly's reply was, 'If there's a choice between being rich and ugly, or poor and good-looking, then rich wins every time.'

Summary

The implications for the future are getting clearer. Services and experiences will become more in demand, maybe at the expense of spending on physical goods. As a consequence, excellent frontline staff will become harder to find and keep.

What is more, the quality of service will become one of the key differentiators of success. If you really wish to delight your customers, then start thinking about what they want. Do it right now!

7: Is There a Secret of Customer Service?

What's actually happening to customer service is quite straightforward. As we saw in Chapter 5, the secret is not that customer service is bad, but that it is harder than it has ever been to deliver good customer service.

 In a world of mass-focused mediocrity, opportunities abound for those people who want to beat the big boys in niches (which the big 'uns aren't interested in).

If companies can't sort their own internal systems and communications, why should they think that they can organise a half-decent call centre? Technology is tough to harness. And customers are increasingly more demanding as their expectations are constantly wooed, courted and conned.

So what?

What's happening is that, despite all the consultants, gurus, outsource experts and evangelists and their rhetoric, the basic fact is that customer service is hard to deliver in the mass economy. This is good news for the smaller business.

If you reflect on some of the recent customer experiences that you have, dare I say, enjoyed, there is usually a striking fact. What is striking is how little it takes to make people happy. I am amazed at how little it takes to 'get it right'. At the same time it is so very difficult to automate or standardise such a process.

At the root of the issue, 'to do it right' doesn't actually require much, but it does require a spark of human intelligence.

The best-kept secret about customer service?

There are some basic things that we must not forget about customer service.

First, service tends to be bad because it really is very hard to do. Try spending a week working as a waiter in a busy restaurant to discover just how difficult it is!

Second, the real (best-kept) secret is to treat the customer as you would like to be treated yourself.

Third, the really hard part of providing excellent customer service is not the service! The really hard part is everything *but* the service! The hard part is to do with how the company thinks about what it is doing and how it behaves as a consequence. Most airlines offer bad service and bad food because they don't actually think of themselves as service organisations: they see themselves as machines for generating revenue from seat miles. Most food outlets don't see themselves as service organisations – they see themselves as burger or pizza factories focusing on profit per employee per hour.

So what?

There is a huge opportunity out there waiting to be snatched up by the likes of you. Many people tolerate the mediocrity that seems to surround them. In fact, many people revel in the 'dumbing down' that is all around them. An abundance of opportunities appear: opportunities to beat the big boys at their own game (because you are so much closer to your customer, so you can give them a truly bespoke service, offering, for example, hand-built skateboards or guitars); opportunities to fill niches that the big boys are not interested in, such as handmade kitchen knives, dog-walking services, one-to-one computer tuition.

Summary

By competing on delivering outstanding customer service you can outplay and outmanoeuvre the big boys. You separate yourself from the competition and can drive customers to your door.

8: Take On the Mindset of a Market Leader

How would you behave if you were the market leader? What would you do differently? How would you be considered by your customers? By your competitors? What would change if you behaved as if you were the market leader?

- The market leader usually does better than the rest.
- To become market leader means that you excel in one of three ways: you take on the mindset of (1) the product leader or (2) the customer-intimate business or (3) the operationally excellent business.
- The art of *'wow!'*

Thought

Don't be a business that sits and waits for the customers to say what they want – rather, create an offering that is so seductive, so compelling, that it virtually demands that customers do business with you.

Behaving like a market leader

Clearly, few of us can become the actual market leader. However, we can behave like a market leader in our narrowly defined niche. Or at least we can model our behaviour on that of a market leader: watch the best, take on their attributes and learn from what they do.

Why would we want to act like a 'market leader'?

The market leader, the number one, the top dog is always remembered – more importantly, they are more profitable and the business will have better long-term prospects. It is more likely still to be around in ten years' time.

So, which are you, 'market leader' or 'follower'? Ask yourself whether you would:

- risk your best product by possibly cannibalising it with a new upgrade
- offer a service at a loss in the hope of establishing a long-term relationship with a client
- enter a joint venture with a direct competitor with the purpose of driving down costs

These are the behaviours of a nimble 'switched-on' market leader. And if the above ideas all seem alien to you, then get used to mediocre performance and constantly playing competitive catch-up.

The smart business will seek to improve its offering continually. To do this it has to make choices. Competitive advantage must be gained in one of three areas.

You can lead by:

- making a better product (for the customer) (**product leadership**)
- being closer to the customer (**customer intimacy**)
- making an even more cost-effective (cheaper) product (for the customer) (**operational excellence**)

If, and it is a big 'if', you are really committed to turning on your customer, then you need to excel in one of these areas and be at least adequate in the other two!

Score yourself

Mark a percentage score for each of the following questions:

1. From the customers' point of view, do you make a better product than your competitors (innovative, excellent)?

0% – 10 – 20 – 30 – 40 – 50 – 60 – 70 – 80 – 90 – 100%
In Your dreams   On a good day   Oh Yes!

2. From the customers' point of view, are you closer to your customers than your competitors (brilliant personal relationships)?

0% – 10 – 20 – 30 – 40 – 50 – 60 – 70 – 80 – 90 – 100%
In Your dreams　　　　　On a good day　　　　　Oh Yes!

3. From the customers' point of view, do you offer an even cheaper/better-value product/service than your competitors?

0% – 10 – 20 – 30 – 40 – 50 – 60 – 70 – 80 – 90 – 100%
In Your dreams　　　　　On a good day　　　　　Oh Yes!

Product leadership

If you focus on product leadership then you are constantly pushing the performance boundaries of your product – and charging the customer for the privilege (premium pricing). In the high street, Nike or Intel is typical of a business that constantly offers newer, better products and as such both lead the market. This can be a tough nut to crack for the smaller business. Mind you, on a smaller scale, Andrew Waterfall's Improvision has used product leadership as its advantage against the competition. Based in Coventry, he offers a constantly updated software product in the narrow field of medical imaging.

Could you take on the behaviours of a product leader?

■ Who is the product leader in your market?
■ What makes them better/smarter/brighter than you?
■ What could you learn from them?

Customer intimacy

Customer intimacy is not just about delivering what the market wants: it is about delivering what *specific customers* want. This is about cultivating relationships, specialising in satisfying unique needs that only the supplier can understand and relate to because of their closeness to the customer. What these businesses are saying is, 'We have the perfect solution for you, and what's more we also have the resources and skills to support and back up the product/service.'

By the very nature of their size and type, large businesses find it difficult to have truly 'intimate' relationships. Service companies or companies in supply chains often practice customer intimacy. Big management consulting houses, for example Andersen Consulting, are known for getting close to their customers, but so are small design agencies such as Interaction, the office designers in Bath.

At a smaller scale, Chris Wiggins, the gardener who makes private domestic gardens 'come alive', gets really close to his customers. He finds out exactly what they like and dislike and finds out what they want to do with their gardens – his experience and first-class people skills enable him to delight his clients with the results that he can produce.

Could you take on the behaviours of a 'customer-intimate' business?

- Who is the Number One at getting really close to the customer in your industry? What makes them better/smarter/brighter than you? What could you learn from them?

- What small change could you implement in your business right now that could make you just two per cent better at getting close to your customer?

- Is there a decision that you could make that might take you, say, five per cent closer to the customer?

Operational excellence

Operationally excellent companies are not primarily product or service innovators, nor do they necessarily develop deep relationships with their customers. What they do is provide middle-of-the-market products at the best prices (with the least inconvenience). Wal-Mart and Asda are good examples of big, no-frills, good-value-to-the-customer businesses. As an example of a smaller business, Binder Wingate offers real operational excellence as a joinery (making things for buildings out of wood) – what's unusual is that its streamlined workshop systems and computer-aided design and manufacturing excellence enable it to make things faster and cheaper than its competitors.

Smaller businesses often find that operational excellence – being the Number One by price – is tough. By definition, larger businesses (even with their larger overheads) gain such significant economies of scale and can command such excellent bulk prices that they can usually deliver a product at a lower price than the smaller business. This is why the price war is so dangerous for the smaller business – on price, Goliath (too) often beats David!

At first, it might appear that a book about the customer is spending a lot of time discussing the operations function, the part of the business that 'does the doing', makes the product or delivers the service. Well, operations is in fact a key part of the whole customer thing – the customer is not the sole domain of the marketing people. We've already seen how the focus on the customer drives all aspects of the business, so let's not forget that the operations department may not be customer-facing as such but it is the fruits of their labours that the customer receives.

Your operations people are part of the team, so don't keep them away from the customers – quite the reverse. Get operations close to the customers so that they can design and make products that the customers really want to use.

Could you take on the behaviours of an 'operationally excellent' business?

- Who is the Number One at being operationally excellent in your industry? What makes them better/smarter/brighter than you? What could you learn from them?
- What small change could you implement in your business right now that could make you just two per cent better at being operationally excellent?
- Is there a decision that you could make that could make you, say, five per cent better at operations?

■ The whole concept of excellence is intriguing. To be mediocre in all fields does imply that your financial results will also be mediocre.

ACTION POINT: Customer-service comparison

Write down a list of companies that are known for the quality of their customer service. Write down no more than two from any one industry. It's best to do this when there is a group of you, so you can aim to get a list of say ten to twenty businesses.

Next, position them against their competitors – are they better than, worse than or about the same as their competitors in terms of standard business measures? The sort of measures that I was thinking of include:

■ profitability
■ return on capital employed
■ market share
■ customer satisfaction
■ staff morale and retention

I think that you get my point. Most businesses that are known for their service also produce above-average results. So, if you want to produce above-average results, you know what you have to do!

Some questions

■ Where can you excel?
■ What business model should you follow? (product leader/ customer intimate/ operational excellence?)
■ If the customer is king, how can you focus your efforts to make the customer feel like royalty?
■ What is the best way for your business?

ACTION POINT: The benefits of a great service strategy

List the potential benefits to your business of getting your service strategy right.

Fast track to improvement: the art of '*wow!*'

What do we mean by 'wow!' You say '*wow!*' when something really impresses you. In business, 'wow!' products have something about them that is unconventional, or fresh or different, or exciting – something electric about them. But it is not just products that can make you go 'wow!' Nearly every step of the product or service process can have a 'wow!' effect.

The recent VW Beetle tries to get as many 'wow!'s as possible into one product by having quirky but innovative styling, promotional materials, details, interior lighting and so on. The first time you sit in the car both explicit and implicit design features assault you – features that make you feel like a 'style god' when you drive the car. 'Wow!' breakthroughs make you more powerful, efficient, effective, productive, valuable and inspiring to your client.

Companies that seek to offer 'wow!' products tend to lead their field (and often charge premium prices for their product). And if you lead and command the business then you should be able to *keep* more business. And if you keep more business then you should be more profitable, if only because you are taking business away from your competitors. More importantly, these innovative companies gain more respect and trust from the customers. (By the way, this is being written on a Sony Vaio laptop – a design icon that I just fell in love with. I am sure that it does the same job as a machine at half the price but it looks and feels so great. More importantly it [a mere computer!] makes me feel good.)

The Same/Better/'Wow!' Index

The Same/Better/'Wow!' Index is a great tool for looking at an existing product or service or for looking at a new one. It is not for the light-hearted because its whole purpose is to get you to design and deliver something extraordinary – so, if you are happy with mediocrity, then this tool is not for you! And, if you are in a situation where you are not really prepared to improve what you offer your customers, then, again, this is not for you.

So, what is this index? It is a simple yet profound tool that can be used in workshops to look at your own product or that of your competitors.

First, you break down your offering into its component parts. You then score each part:

- ■ 'same' – no better than (probably about the same as) the competition
- ■ 'better' – something that is probably a little better than that provided by your competitors
- ■ 'wow!' – really amazing in some sense; it takes your breath away

Case study: Creating 'wow!'

A cursory glance at management training programmes makes you realise that they are all 'much of a muchness' – they all claim to improve your profitability by making you a better businessperson or by giving you some advantage but somehow there still seems to be a gap between the marketing hype and what you get.

Designing a new, so-called better programme, Jim McPherson realised that all training programmes do look about the same. A visit to the Annual Training Providers' Conference convinced him of the fact: rows of stands with photos of teams working together in the tug-of-war or abseiling; all the companies claiming that their product was bespoke, tailored, individual and responsive. The rhetoric was so severe as to be depressing.

Jim set out to design a new programme. First he outlined his design and started to draft out the marketing materials and so forth. Next, he used the Same/Better/'Wow!' Index to calibrate the offering that he was designing. His score sheet looked as follows:

Based on how I envisage running the new training programme I score the product as follows:

THE SAME/BETTER/'WOW!' INDEX

Component:	Same	Better	Wow!
Marketing materials		😐	
Quality of telesales	🙁		
Quality of email communication	🙁		
Joining instructions	🙁		
Pre-course worksheet		😐	
Administration	🙁		
Welcome at the venue	🙁		
Signposting at the venue	🙁		
Venue hospitality	🙁		
Speaker presentations		😐	
Speaker–audience contact		😐	
Ideas/concepts/course content			😊
Handout materials		😐	
Visuals	🙁		
Post-course follow-up	🙁		
Changes in delegate behaviour	🙁		
Changes in delegate's business performance	🙁		

Jim scored the Index as above – he realised that his course wasn't particularly different from anything else that was being offered. In fact, he was actually following in the footsteps of a long line of thoroughly mediocre and pretty unmemorable courses. This index spurred him on to figure out what he would have to do to get at least a third of the scores in the 'Wow!' column and less than a third in the 'same' column.

After several days of furious brainstorming and programme design, Jim finally came across a formula that really did create an exceptional programme, scoring six 'wow!'s, eight 'better's and three 'same's, Jim had created a powerhouse programme. It looked, felt and was different from the standard training offering. Using the Index had driven Jim to create something that would excite and ignite the excitement in his delegates – like others, he had to recognise that he wasn't being original enough before he could break through his ordinary thinking to create something a little bit special.

Using the Index

- forced Jim to create a better product
- informed all aspects of the programme design
- meant Jim had a tool to motivate everyone involved in the creation and delivery of the new product

When talking about the process, Jim observes: 'The Index is not about creating change for change's sake – that would be a waste of time. No, when you use the Index you must see it as a tool to make a quantum leap in your thinking – to help you to deliver outstanding products. Outstanding products stand out, sell more and are more profitable – that's my idea of a win–win situation!'

ACTION POINT: How do *you* perform?

Consider your worst performing product or service. Using the Index template below, decide the key components, and then score each of the components. How do you perform? (You may need an extra column to score where you are worse than the competition!) Taking each component, think of three things that you could do to improve the performance. Even better, do this exercise with a customer.

Next, take your best product or service and map out its scores. What are the areas that you are consistently scoring well in? What themes are emerging about what you are good at or where you delight customers? Always look at this exercise through the customers' eyes. What learning points do you take away from this? And what are you going to do as a result?

THE SAME/BETTER/'WOW!' INDEX

Component	Same	Better	Wow!

Using the 'wow!' steps

Having identified the steps in your business process, you could try to come up with at least two alternative ways or approaches to these activities. At every single step look for the incremental improvement as well as the big step changes. But first . . .

A gentle reminder

Business books can be wonderful things to read, but if you just want a good read then I suggest that you go to the fiction department at your local bookstore. If you want to make a difference to the performance of your business then you will have to change the way that you do certain things. If you read this book and do not change at least one thing about the way that you run your business, then you have wasted your time.

Action points have been put in the book to be done – please do work on them. Write in the book or in the margins – do not be precious about it. Do not kid yourself that you will come back to the action points when you need to – we rarely do that. Make a conscious effort to get engaged and use the exercises in the book to look at your business. The process of stepping back and looking at your business will make you consider the business in a different light. It is this change in perspective that very often gives you the 'eureka!' moment. But you won't get any great insights unless you at least make the effort to look for new or better ways of running your business. End of lecture!

ACTION POINT: Getting to 'wow!'

Come up with fifty 'wow!' or breakthrough ideas for your business process. You've got thirty minutes in which to do it.

- Identify **twenty opportunities** that your business has not exploited.
- List **twenty decisions** that you were going to make but haven't got around to yet. What's the consequence of your procrastination?
- List as many **'wow!'/breakthroughs** that other industries have had. Can you take anything from these for your business?

Benefits of running a great 'wow!' business

Some of the benefits of running a 'wow!' business will include:

- better staff morale
- lower staff turnover
- better staff retention
- more effective staff training
- more repeat business
- more referrals
- higher prices
- better margins
- a business that you can be proud of

Quite an impressive list.

Summary

Do you have the mindset of the market leader, or are you just a follower? Followers tend to achieve average profits and average growth. Can you afford to be mediocre? I think not. A new mind-set shakes up your thoughts and gets things moving. Try it!

More importantly, it is your duty to figure out how to really satisfy your customers – if you can get them to say 'wow!' when they look at your service then you are probably doing the right stuff. You cannot afford for them to look at your product and shrug their shoulders.

9: What You Need to
Know About Marketing
(that your marketing team
may not know)

*This is the stuff you need to know to put together an informed and
coherent plan to put the customer at the centre of your efforts. The
following 'audit' looks at the customer in the context of the other
parts of the marketing scheme.*

■ A marketing audit.

It's crunch time for marketing professionals and their industry. In
larger businesses, marketers have got away with hiding behind their
trendy suits and PR budgets for much too long. It is time to sort
them out once and for all. If you employ one of these so-called
experts, someone responsible for marketing, then drag them into
your office and get them to answer some of the questions that follow this case study.

Case study: Pat's dilemma

A new government agency was set up to deliver a specific
educational and training product to a particular segment of
the small-business market. The target audience was very specific and its needs were particular to the industry that it was
in.

It was charged with being an independently run and truly
commercial outfit, and the chief executive, Pat, confided in me
that she was virtually pulling her hair out. I will transcribe the
general drift of her angst-ridden conversation with me.

'Marketing people have no clue around here ... They think that their job is to spend down the budget ... they nod their heads when I ask if they understand my vision for the business ... I think that they understand the words, but they don't really understand what it is that I am trying to achieve ... they put together inappropriate offerings that we cannot deliver on ... And every time they make a promise on our behalf (that we can't match) then our credibility in front of the customer diminishes ... we shoot ourselves in the foot endlessly ... we don't need any competition to challenge our position ...We are losing our credibility without any help from anyone else – we are doing it all by ourselves. The business looks foolish, probably incompetent. To be honest I'd rather put the money in a bonfire and burn it rather than spend it badly ... at least if we had a bonfire, passers-by get the benefit from the heat ...'

Pat is absolutely correct. Until her marketing department understands what it is that Pat is trying to do, who it is that she is trying to delight and why and how, then most of the marketing effort is in vain.

Auditing the marketing people!

In *Kick-Start Your Business*, I proposed a marketing audit, and I am extending it here. I am doing this as a starting point to stimulate answers to the questions below.

If your marketing expert fails to come up with succinct answers for any of the following, then it would suggest to me that they are not really doing their job properly. I suggest that you reduce their salary by ten per cent for each question poorly answered – a total of fifteen questions means that some marketers will end up paying you so they can work for you. So, here goes, fifteen questions every marketer should be able to answer for the business that they work in.

1. What drives your **industry**?
2. What drives your **market**?

- Who are the key players in the market (today and tomorrow)?
- What determines the nature of the market?
- What are the trends and benchmarks of performance within the market?
- What are the key influences on the market?

3. Who are your **competitors**?

- Who are your competitors today?
- Who will be your competitors tomorrow?
- What are their strengths, weaknesses, opportunities and threats?
- What are they trying to achieve in the short run? In the long run?
- What will their next move be? When?
- What is their Unique Selling Proposition (USP)?
- How do other competitors perceive them?
- How do the customers perceive them?

4. Who are your **customers**?

- Who are your customers today?
- Who are your customers tomorrow?
- Why do they buy the product and/or service?
- Why do they buy from you? When?
- Why do they leave you?
- How do they use the product and/or service?
- How do they buy? How often? Where? Who?
- Who uses the product and/or service?

5. How do your **target customers** behave?
6. How good are you, **yourselves**?

- How good is your performance to date (finance, marketing and operations)?
- What is your potential (resources, experience, controls, ideas and innovation and leadership)?

> - What are your weaknesses? Your opportunities?
> - What are your threats? Your strengths?
> - How good are you, really?

If you put together these six stages of the Marketing Audit, you should have a pretty clear idea of what your capabilities are and also what your opportunities are.

Marketing is the process of targeting your product or service to satisfy customer needs in the most cost-effective (and profitable) way. As our organisations are confronted with exponentially increasing rates of change at every level, we need to step back and ask ourselves some fundamental questions about our products and services.

7. What is the need that must be satisfied?

> - Who has the need?
> - What do they need it for?
> - Who does the buying? When do they buy? Why?
> - What will influence the need?
> - How will it change?

8. What are the products or services that will satisfy it?

> - What particular aspects of the product/service are important?
> - What is it that customers are buying?
> - What are the product features?
> - What are the product benefits?
> - At what price?

9. How are the need and the product best connected?

> - How is your identity branded/perceived?
> - How are the product/services branded?
> - How is it packaged?
> - How is it promoted?

> ■ How is it sold?
> ■ How is it available?

Like any other strategy, your strategy for marketing is your route map for getting there. So, the fundamental question you need to address is, what is there? In other words,

Why . . . will **which** customers . . . choose **you?**

Quite simply, you need to be able to answer the following and write down your answers:

10. What is your market position now, and in the future?
11. What is your customer position now and in the future?
12. How will you achieve and sustain this new position?

Essentially, you are trying to create a product offering, or more specifically a brand. If you wish to create this brand you need to ask some further questions to establish, in relation to customer needs and any competitive offerings (brands), what is the positioning in the customers' minds that you have or, rather, would like to have? A good starting point is to define:

13. To whom does the brand appeal?
14. What does the brand offer?
15. Why is it better than other offerings?

If you can answer these questions – and it is no mean task to address them – then you are a long way towards being able to define your marketing vision and hence your strategy to achieve it.

Summary

Armed with the right information you can make informed and educated decisions. Without this information you are making wild stabs in the dark. The gathering of the information does not need to be a lifetime's work, but it will help you make better decisions.

10: Working the Law of the Vital Few

Cut the deadwood. Do the stuff that matters. Or be a busy fool.

> - How does the Law of the Vital Few apply to your business and that of your customer?
> - How does the Law of the Trivial Many apply to your business and that of your customer?

Question

What would happen if you 'sacked' 80 per cent of your least profitable customers and worked more with the rest, the profitable ones?

The 80:20 Principle, also known as Pareto's Principle, is a classic of management science. In fact, it is such a classic that most people have forgotten all about it. Writing in the late nineteenth century, the Paris-born Italian economist and sociologist Vilfredo Pareto (1848–1923) noticed that, with amazing regularity, things were not distributed evenly. A few people earned the majority of the money; a few people possessed most of the wealth; a few animals were larger than the rest. This has been translated into the 80:20 rule.

Fact

Twenty per cent of inputs cause eighty per cent of outputs. The 80:20 rule in business says that 20 per cent of salespeople get 80 per cent of your sales; 20 per cent of your customers deliver 80 per cent of your profit; 20 per cent of your time creates 80 per cent of your outputs. This is the Law of the Vital Few and the Trivial Many.

So what?

The implications of the Pareto Principle are several for your business. The upside of the principle is that some of your inputs are incredibly effective. For instance, 20 per cent of suppliers deliver 80 per cent of your supplies.

On the other hand, Pareto also implies incredible inefficiencies. For example, the other 20 per cent of your supplies (a fraction, really) are delivered by 80 per cent of your suppliers (the majority).

If you play the 80 : 20 rule to your advantage, then you can:

- **focus** on what works
- **recognise** that you can become progressively less effective
- **concentrate** on the vital few and try to cut the trivial many – focus on becoming more effective (otherwise you will become the proverbial busy fool)

And what you *won't* be doing is chasing the perfect solution. The more time you spend on a problem, the less value you add, so it is better to do the big stuff, the powerful thinking, and getting the right basic shape to a solution rather than always concentrating on the detail, the minutiae, which may not be the most effective use of your time – unless, of course, that is what you are paid to do.

Case study

Fastbake looked at its customer database and segmented the list according to profitability. As if by magic, my words were true: 80 per cent of contribution to profit came from just six customers. With a total contribution to profit of $17 million, the top six generated a staggering $13.6 million. The other customers, generally much smaller, numbered some 20 and contributed just under $2.5 million. The senior team could not believe how the Pareto Principle was played out in their business – the law of the vital few and the trivial many sang out to them!

Action point: Applying the 80 : 20 rule

Draw up a list of your customers. Order them according to revenues generated. And order them according to contribution generated. In either case, does the 80 : 20 rule apply? Do 20 per cent of inputs generate 80 per cent of outputs? If so, what are you going to do about it?

Draw up a list of your salespeople. Order them according to revenues generated. And order them according to contribution generated. Does the 80 : 20 rule apply? If so, what are you going to do about it?

What's this got to do with the customer?

For the customer, 80 per cent of products come from 20 per cent of suppliers. Can you get your business into that Top 20 Per Cent list?

For the customer, 80 per cent of their profitable activity takes place in 20 per cent of their time. Can you help them to increase the size of the Vital Few? Can you help the customer to reduce the size of their Trivial Many?

Don't always look for perfect solutions. The 80 : 20 rule tells us that we achieve pretty good results very rapidly. The thing that takes the time is the polishing and refining of the ideas. Yet the key issue is getting the fundamentals, the architecture sorted.

▌ Summary

The 80 : 20 rule can be applied to your business and its use can generate astounding results. Often overlooked, it is worth spending a bit of time seeing how you can use 80 : 20 thinking to improve your business.

11: Creating 'Customer Pull' – Buzz, Buzz, Buzz!

> ■ Interruption marketing no longer works – word-of-mouth referral is now more effective than a big advertising campaign.
>
> ■ Your business needs to create a buzz of its own, and that will draw people towards it.

The old style of marketing no longer works. That world ran along the following, outdated principles:

1. The company advertises (the method: to interrupt the customer while he or she is walking, watching TV, listening to the radio . . .).
2. The customer sees the advertisement (is interrupted).
3. The customer buys the product.

This is no longer how it happens. Wake up and smell the coffee! Advertising is everywhere – customers become numb to advertising messages as the specially crafted messages become so much white noise. Increasingly, advertising spend is less and less effective.

Fact

More and more, a critical part of marketing is word-of-mouth sales. Validation from important personal relationships is key to the customer's buying process; and yet most marketers remain ignorant of, or at best oblivious to, the power of word-of-mouth referrals and sales. The customer is now at the centre of these relationships.

Fact

David Maister, in his splendid book *Managing the Professional Service Firm*, cites research that claims that over 50 per cent of new clients come via the referrals route. In other words, the majority of new clients do not come from advertising, brochures, conferences and so forth. Interestingly enough, the budget for nonreferrals may be in the region of ten per cent of revenues, whereas the budget to develop referrals may be zero! Seems like a golden opportunity here, waiting to be taken.

Buzz, buzz, buzz

Great products have a 'buzz' factor – people talk about them and are excited by them. The 'buzz' factor can be created or nurtured. The thinking is that the more buzz your product has, the more sales you will make. Wouldn't it be great if everyone were talking about your product (and not your competitor's)?

Question

Can you think of a way to get people talking about you or your product?

Question

On a scale of one to ten, how would you rate your business in terms of the buzz that it generates?

The quantity of buzz that can be generated is dependent on the nature of the product itself. It is a lot harder to create a buzz about a dull product, although that could be challenged now that Ben & Jerry's and Häagen-Dazs have lifted ice cream out of the doldrums, and even milk and electricity are now being branded in the UK.

There should be a direct correlation between buzz, success and profitability. I don't have academic evidence to support this idea but it does seem intuitively correct to me. After all, with enough buzz, your product should virtually jump off the shelves and into your customer's shopping trolley.

What determines the strength of buzz

While the following list is far from definitive, it does suggest key factors that determine the level of buzz about your product/service. Is it:

- exciting, 'to fall in love with', 'to die for' – the latest executive toy?
- innovative – Google.com?
- personal experience – books, airlines, cars?
- complex – software, medical procedures?
- expensive – computers, shoes?
- observable – clothes, cars, phones?

Question
What is it that makes your product buzz?

Question
What gives it the 'wow!' factor?

Question
How could you turn up the volume, increase the colour intensity, make the message louder or increase the strength of feelings that people have about your product?

ACTION POINT: Test your buzz

Take your service or one of your products. Score it on its 'buzz' factor.

Is your product exciting?

0% – 10 – 20 – 30 – 40 – 50 – 60 – 70 – 80 – 90 – 100%
In your dreams   On a good day   Oh, yes!

Is it innovative?

0% – 10 – 20 – 30 – 40 – 50 – 60 – 70 – 80 – 90 – 100%
In your dreams   On a good day   Oh, yes!

Can your product be used or considered as a personal experience?

0% – 10 – 20 – 30 – 40 – 50 – 60 – 70 – 80 – 90 – 100%
In your dreams   On a good day   Oh, yes!

Is it apparently quite simple and yet complex?

0% − 10 − 20 − 30 − 40 − 50 − 60 − 70 − 80 − 90 − 100%
In your dreams   On a good day   Oh, yes!

Is it expensive?

0% − 10 − 20 − 30 − 40 − 50 − 60 − 70 − 80 − 90 − 100%
In your dreams   On a good day   Oh, yes!

Is it observable – is its use relatively conspicuous?

0% − 10 − 20 − 30 − 40 − 50 − 60 − 70 − 80 − 90 − 100%
In your dreams   On a good day   Oh, yes!

How did you score?
A few thoughts, again:

- Can you think of any area where you could have done better?
- Can you think of anything that you could do this week, or even today, that could improve any of your scores?
- What's holding you back from getting on with these actions?

Case study: Napster.com

Napster.com, the website for downloading free music for MP3 players, created a terrific buzz.

Question: Is the product exciting?

Answer: Oh, yes – new music for free!

Question: Is it innovative?

Answer: Oh, yes – never been done before.

Question: Can the product be used for or considered as a personal experience?

Answer: Oh, yes – you select according to your own taste.

Question: Is it expensive?

Answer: No – quite the opposite! But what you got was of high value.

Question: Is it observable – is its use relatively conspicuous?

Answer: Yes – you get your friends to listen to your latest download and tell them all about Napster at the same time!

Summary

Buzz is part of the process of getting things 'turned on'. If you know how to excite customers (and do this profitably) then you have discovered (or created) a remarkable formula for success.

12: Infecting Your Customers to Help You

What you want is your product's reputation to spread rapidly, by word of mouth and with negligible cost to yourself. Even if the word 'infect' has some unpleasant connotations, the way that a virus spreads (carried by hosts) is analogous to how you would like to see your reputation spread.

- Word of mouth that spreads like a virus – viral marketing.
- Systematic viral marketing – permission marketing.
- One-to-one – a radical approach to being more profitable.
- And good old-fashioned referrals.

'Viral marketing' has been heralded as the 'way of the future'. What was so exciting about the concept of viral marketing was that it was spawned by the late nineties dotcom gold rush.

In essence, the idea is simple yet deceptively powerful: if you have a product with a good buzz factor then it should market itself. Because we live in a very networked world, if you produce a product or service that is attractive to the network then the network will talk about your offering and do the marketing for you. In fact, if you have a really sexy product then the network will do all the work for you.

The message is carried by a 'host' for free. The host meets potential customers who become potential 'hosts' who will also carry the message to others. And because ten people contact ten people who contact ten people, the numbers stack up very quickly (as they do in multilevel marketing).

The 'host' is nearly always a willing participant in the proceedings. They are flattered to be associated with their virus and they are often protagonists who positively celebrate the benefits of the virus offering.

Examples of viral marketing

Yahoo! is often quoted as a classic case of viral marketing. Every email sent by a Yahoo! subscriber has a strapline attached at the bottom saying that the email was sent via Yahoo! and inviting the reader to join for free. The message gets spread very quickly and reaches the precise target audience.

Amazon.com is another example. Early users of Amazon.com were real fans – the early adopters we mentioned earlier on. The website for books was a genuine first of its kind. It was cheap, had a vast stock and was cool. Amazon.com created an 'affiliate' programme. Affiliates could sign up to sell books via Amazon.com – with the application of some novel programming anyone could send one of their own website visitors to the Amazon site; Amazon would know that you had sent them and you receive a commission on sales. To see an example of this, go to my website at www.robert-craven.com and you will see how the site links straight through to the Amazon site.

The Amazon model grew explosively. People positively wanted to be associated with the new business. Amazon had reached 'movers and shakers', who sang the praises of the business from the metaphorical rooftops – people were positively evangelical. And people who became affiliates promoted the site (and got paid in the process).

Clearly the best recommendation for a product is an existing user, and ideally someone who is not being paid to endorse the product. Sometimes this does happen.

The introduction of the hi-tech yo-yo was a classic of offline viral marketing. Yo-yos were distributed to ten- to twelve-year-olds. The children were even shown how to do fancy tricks with them. And what happened next became a real business success. The children (the hosts/carriers) took the yo-yos to school. At school, others saw the yo-yo tricks and were desperate to get a yo-yo of their own. When asked where they came from, the host pointed the desperate onlooker towards the only local supplier, who not only sold the yo-yos but gave free yo-yo lessons, so more and more trained-up children took yo-yos to school, which fuelled the demand in others and so forth. This is buzz in action.

Permission marketing

'Permission marketing', a phrase coined by Seth Godin in his book of the same name, is a derivative of viral marketing. It takes advantage of the use of networks; more importantly it exploits the willingness of certain people to be involved in your product or business.

How does it work?

You ask people if they mind if you offer them something for nothing (in return for you acquiring their [email] address). At the same time you ask for a positive sign that they wish to receive the freebie. In other words, they *opt in* to receiving future mailings. This is important: if you allow people only to *opt out* then what you are doing is called sending 'spam', or unsolicited mail. Once you have people's permission to communicate with them, you can send them subsequent targeted offers.

The philosophy behind 'permission marketing' is as follows. When potential clients have invited you to communicate with them, they are very receptive (whereas most uninvited junk mail never even gets read). The audience must be very targeted and you must not waste their time – you must offer them something they want. Because of the opt-in nature of the list, the only people who will have signed up are people who are interested (to some degree) in what you do – they are warm leads. Ideally, you start by offering free services and progressively you offer increasingly higher-value items. You convince the client of your credibility with the free items and then you drive them towards your better-value/higher-priced products. The target moves through a cycle from being a stranger to a friend to a customer to a *loyal* customer.

Case study:

Eliza Principe, the sales manager at JCJ Training, had over four thousand names in her database – people who had been on courses or made enquiries or people with whom she had communicated over the last three years. She had been obsessive about collecting the addresses.

STEP 1 – invite to opt in and receive free survey

Eliza sent an email to all four thousand names on her database inviting people to sign up to receive a free (old) survey on 'Getting the Most from Training – How to Take the Learning into the Workplace'. The results: 500 names did not exist/had died; 2,500 opted in and wanted to receive the survey; 500 asked to be taken off the mailing list and 500 did not reply at all. So, 2,500 surveys were sent out by email, mainly to training managers and purchasers.

STEP 2 – invite to receive free chapter

The 2,500 opt-ins were invited to receive a copy of a sample chapter from the JCJ's guru/managing director's forthcoming book. Of the 2,500, 1,500 asked for a copy. So, out of the original 4,000 names she now had 1,500 'very interested' people.

STEP 3 – invite to seminar

The 1,500 very interested people were now invited to a free seminar. JCJ knew that these people were interested in the subject and were familiar with the house style. Out of 1,500 people invited to the free seminar, 90 signed up to attend

STEP 4 – run seminar and start to sell programmes

Of the 90 who signed up for the seminar, 65 actually attended; 45 people bought seminars as a result of attending. Initial sales to the value of £65,000 were made on that day! Over the coming year these 65 people bought a further £390,000 of training and made referrals to the value of £170,000.

This result came from using a simple email system with a simple database. All materials were 'free' – pamphlets had been printed and were ready to be pulped; everything else was sent by electronic means. The only real cost was the time inputting, preparing and sending emails.

And the 'trick' is that you are talking only to interested people, as defined by them. So you waste little effort trying to persuade people who would never be interested in your offering.

Step 1 – invite to opt in and receive free survey

Out	4,000
Dead	500
Positive replies	2,500
Negative replies	500
No replies	500

Step 2 – invite to receive free chapter

Out	2,500
Positive replies	1,500
Negative replies	500
No replies	500

Step 3 – invite to seminar

Out	1,500
Positive replies	90
Negative replies	400
No replies	500

Step 4 – run seminar and start to sell programmes

Invitations accepted	90
Attended	65
Actual sales	45
Sales on the day	£65,000
Subsequent sales	£390,000
Referral value	£130,000
Year 1 income	£585,000

Other benefits of permission marketing

The story as described above fails to mention other benefits of running a permission-marketing campaign. For instance, you can return to the 'negative replies' or 'no replies' and try to make contact with them again.

If you are able to personalise the emails you send (for example, to say 'Dear Paul' or whatever), then the response rates increase dramatically. You can personalise the emails 'by hand' or automatically (talk to a 'tech-head' about it!). With personalisation, the recipients actually start to respond positively. Feeling that they are being communicated with on a one-to-one basis, recipients will make comments such as 'Thanks for sending me . . .' and 'I will look at what you sent me over the weekend.' The clever marketer will respond as an individual. This increases the speed of the development of rapport between the customer and your company. If the customers feel comfortable with how you communicate and the messages that you are sending, both explicit and implicit, then you will find it easy to start a real dialogue. From the dialogue, you will get feedback about your products and those of your competitors; you will find out what the client really would like you to do and what it is that you do that irritates them. Not only does the client feel in charge but they also behave almost like a friend, and this increases the likelihood not only of a sale, but more importantly of a longer-term relationship with someone who will tell others about how responsive you have been.

Question
Is permission marketing pure manipulation?

Answer
If used with a mischievous intent, then yes. But, if a permission-marketing campaign is set up with the intention of getting closer to customers in order to help them, then no.

One-to-one – a radical approach to customers

Here's an approach that is not for the faint-hearted but it is worth spending twenty minutes talking it through with your senior team. One-to-one marketing refers to the concept of focusing on fewer customers, but developing a much deeper relationship. Big businesses find it really tough to appear to market convincingly from one person to another person. The smaller business finds this much easier to do because often it really is one-to-one marketing.

In many instances, the intimacy of the one-to-one relationship is far more profitable than the mailshot anonymity of so many marketing departments. Could this be the case for you?

Question

What would happen if you 'sacked', say, the least profitable 60 per cent of your customers?

1. You would be rid of the unprofitables.
2. You would have only profitable clients left (so you would be more profitable).
3. You would have removed most of your 'difficult' clients (the customers from hell).
4. You would have less than half the work to do, requiring less than half the resources – your costs would crash; your profits would soar.
5. You would be left with clients who were less price-sensitive and happier with your offering.
6. You could now seek to get a bigger share of the wallets of your remaining clients.

Good old-fashioned referrals

A simple action to get more business: increase the number of customers by increasing the number of referrals. Sometimes we are so busy looking for new customers that we forget the tried and tested methods of finding and developing additional sales. This is a list of different places to go to look for referrals:

1. Ask current clients.
2. Ask past clients (why do they not deal with you now?).

3. Review and revisit unconverted prospects.
4. Refer unconverted prospects to a competitor (and get a finder's fee!).
5. Pass leads to/from other companies outside your physical area.
6. Ask advertising salespeople whom they know who may be interested in your product/service.
7. Seek the assistance of all the professionals you deal with (banker, accountant, solicitor . . .).
8. Work on your affinity groups (how do you get to the rest of a sector?).
9. Don't forget your own business contacts and their contacts.
10. And don't forget members of the various clubs and societies that you belong to.
11. Ask people in your parent company or subsidiary companies if appropriate.
12. Don't forget associated/sister companies.
13. Talk to people in your strategic alliances.
14. Talk to friends.
15. Talk to relations.
16. Contact local business clubs/business links etc.
17. Talk to magazine journalists/editors.
18. Talk to your PR company.
19. Talk to whoever else benefits when you succeed (staff, suppliers).
20. Contact associations of all the above (e.g. accountants' printer).

Summary

A responsibly run permission-marketing or viral-marketing campaign can radically improve your profitability. Not only is it relatively inexpensive to run, but it is hugely effective. These techniques get you close to your customer – from a more powerful point of view, you get the customers who want to work with you to become close to you.

13: If Customer Experience is Everything, Then What is it?

See through the customer's eyes. Use customer-experience audits.

> ■ The customer-experience audits.

Customer-experience audits are incredibly difficult to run. They are different from the usual customer-satisfaction surveys. Customer satisfaction does not tell us enough: what matters is not that we are satisfactory, but whether the customer will be loyal to us. As a result, it is crucial to understand what it feels like to be one of your customers. And there are only two ways to do this. Ask your customers what it feels like and be a customer (or pretend to be the customer).

ACTION POINT: The line between love and hate

Here's an interesting little exercise that I find really thought provoking. Draw up a list of your top ten or twenty customers. Score them on a scale between love and hate. Whom do you love? Whom do you hate? Why? Should you be working with them at all if you hate them? Whom are you helping by doing that? How much angst do they cause you?

The customer-experience audit

> We stay close to the customer at every stage of their experience.
>
> 0% – 10 – 20 – 30 – 40 – 50 – 60 – 70 – 80 – 90 – 100%
> In your dreams   On a good day   Absolutely!

We create memorable 'wow!' encounters that inspire them to spread the legend to other potential customers.

0% − 10 − 20 − 30 − 40 − 50 − 60 − 70 − 80 − 90 − 100%
In your dreams   On a good day   Absolutely!

We positively touch customers with the pride that we invest in our work.

0% − 10 − 20 − 30 − 40 − 50 − 60 − 70 − 80 − 90 − 100%
In your dreams   On a good day   Absolutely!

We demonstrate superior levels of empathy for the customers' situation and needs.

0% − 10 − 20 − 30 − 40 − 50 − 60 − 70 − 80 − 90 − 100%
In your dreams   On a good day   Absolutely!

We have created systems that are intuitively loved by customers − far more than just customer-friendly.

0% − 10 − 20 − 30 − 40 − 50 − 60 − 70 − 80 − 90 − 100%
In your dreams   On a good day   Absolutely!

Infect your staff

People act spontaneously from the belief that delighting customers is their real job.

0% − 10 − 20 − 30 − 40 − 50 − 60 − 70 − 80 − 90 − 100%
In your dreams   On a good day   Got it!

Customers feel like partners; staff feel like partners − this is not simply about 'service level' agreements.

0% − 10 − 20 − 30 − 40 − 50 − 60 − 70 − 80 − 90 − 100%
In your dreams   On a good day   Got it!

We have a culture where people find real pleasure in giving service to others.

0% − 10 − 20 − 30 − 40 − 50 − 60 − 70 − 80 − 90 − 100%
In your dreams   On a good day   Got it!

We have generated an unstoppable belief in our people that they can invent their own future rather than be restrained by outside forces.

0% − 10 − 20 − 30 − 40 − 50 − 60 − 70 − 80 − 90 − 100%
In your dreams   On a good day   Got it!

Customer experience

You know what the customer experience is; you are a customer for so much of the time, buying shoes, food, a car or whatever. So how do you want your customer to feel?

ACTION POINT: A starter for ten

Take a blank sheet of paper and a pen. Imagine how you would like your customers to feel after they have bought something from you. Below I've used the example of getting your car serviced by Kevin.

Write down a list of twenty words to describe how you would like them to feel. As you can see, coming up with five or ten words is quite easy but looking for a whole twenty is pretty tough.

For instance:

- 'Happy.'
- 'Confident.'
- 'Pleased.'
- 'Delighted.'
- 'Ready to book in the next service.'
- 'It was free of hassle.'
- 'Good value for money.'

Now, think of phrases that the customer might say to their partner about the experience. I've put some examples down below:

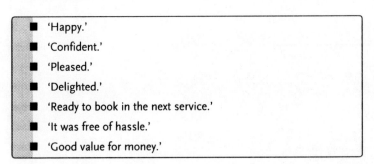

- 'It was great getting the car from Kevin.'
- 'Kevin's a good bloke.'
- 'Kevin gave me incredible value for money.'
- 'I'm not quite sure what Kevin's done, but it all seems OK.'
- 'Kevin's made my car look like new.'
- 'Kevin went to the trouble of polishing the car.'

And what are the phrases that you would want them to be saying when they leave your business:

- 'I'll never take my car anywhere else.'
- 'Kevin really knows what he is doing.'
- 'We must get Kevin a Christmas present.'
- Kevin must be the best garage mechanic we've ever used.'

Summary

The more you can visualise what you want people to say about your business, the more you can start to fill the gap between your desired state and the current state. You need to understand what the business looks like through the customer's eyes.

14: Presenting Your Product, Presenting Your Business

Would you buy a CD without its cover? Do you just buy 'music' when you buy a CD or is there more to it? This brief chapter asks you to think a little about packaging.

- Be aware of the importance of the package as well as its contents.
- Branding isn't just for the big businesses.
- Key questions in branding.
- How do you differ from your competition – positioning yourself.

Question
From the customer's point of view, how important is packaging?

Opinion
In my opinion, there are a number of cases where the packaging really adds to the customer's experience. So, if you want to help the customer to feel as if he (or she) were king (or queen), then you had better think carefully about packaging – and I refer to packaging in the loosest possible sense to mean anything that accompanies the product or service (not just the box that it is supplied in).

When we buy a product, it normally comes in a package that adds value to the product itself. Old record covers are often considered to be almost as important as the music itself. They add to customers' experience although customers think they are buying only music. Likewise CD jewel boxes add to the experience of the listener. In other words, when someone buys a CD, they actually buy a whole lot more: the print and messages on the CD, the cover notes and so forth are all part of an implicit package.

If you want to take the argument further, packaging can actually represent something that no longer exists – we keep the champagne cork many years after the event or we keep a wedding dress because it is the only tangible thing that we have left that represents a happy event.

So . . .
I guess that the learning point is that you should not underestimate the value of packaging – more significantly, you need to know when to sell the content and not the wrapper.

Question
Is branding only for big businesses?

Fact
Brand clutter creates a 'brand overload'. American consumers are confronted with 35 varieties of bagels, 66 sub-brands of General Motors and more than 13,000 mutual funds – isn't it time to simplify the whole thing?

Whole books are written about brands and the impact of brands on customers and on culture. Branding is not simply the playground of trendy consumer items such as trainers, jeans and drinks. The emphasis is nearly always on the well-known, big businesses.

Caterpillar, the tractor manufacturers, now sell boots and backpacks. Intel, the computer-parts people, hardly make a sexy product, but we all know who they are and we know their adverts. And if Caterpillar and Intel can brand themselves then surely anyone can!

It can be argued that the exponential growth in wealth and cultural influence of the multinationals (at the end of the twentieth century) can be traced back to one idea developed by management theorists in the mid-nineteen eighties. That idea was that successful corporations must primarily produce brands rather than products. Until then, the brand was recognised as important, but the product itself had always been thought to be more important.

Nike, Apple, Calvin Klein, Disney, Levi's and Starbucks emerged in the eighties and branding was becoming a much larger focus for their businesses. The Body Shop, the Gap and IKEA promoted what could be described as 'experiential' shopping environments.

Scott Bedbury of Starbucks in the *New York Times* (20/10/97) recognised that 'consumers don't truly believe there's a huge difference between products', which is why brands must 'establish emotional ties' with their customers, such as the 'Starbucks Experience'. He goes on to say that Starbucks customers don't queue up just for coffee. 'It's the romance of the coffee experience, the feeling of warmth and community that people get in Starbucks stores.'

While we see and read about big-business brands, the concept can be used to the advantage of the smaller business.

What can the smaller businesses learn?

Branding is all about how we communicate. To be more precise, it is about *what* we communicate.

You leak messages like radioactivity. Your business leaks messages all the time. The way that you answer the phone, how you address envelopes, your logo, your car park, the quality of your headed notepaper – all these things convey messages to your customers, to your competitors and to your staff.

You cannot *not* communicate. Everything you do says something about how you behave. And, if that is the case, then you can set about designing and planning how and what you wish to communicate.

Key questions in branding

- To whom are you trying to communicate?
- What are you trying to convey?
- How will you know if you have been successful?

So what?

The emergence of brand before product plays into your hands if you can seize the opportunity. On the one hand you can learn from how the 'big boys' have behaved – you can brand your product and service. On the other hand you can play judo with their huge scale and lack of flexibility and turn their strength to your advantage.

The large businesses are out to destroy the competition; they are out to increase their market share; they are out to get business from the majority. They are not particularly interested in the minorities and the niches: big businesses want big wins from big audiences. More importantly, their 'machine' is obsessed with continual growth, a form of perpetual growth chasing world domination. All this leaves plenty of space for you to work and grow your business as long as you don't compete head-on.

Case study: Moods Restaurant

For years Moods has traded using the strapline 'The Town's Best-Kept Secret'. Carole, the owner still works the restaurant in Brighton most nights with her French husband. Big-brand restaurants have come and gone over the last decade or so, because they thought that the streets of their tourist-infested town were paved with gold.

For Carole the formula has been relatively straightforward: an obsession with offering good, well-cooked food, the creation of friendly ambience and a recognition that people, both customers and staff, are everything in a service industry. The whole operation depends on the effective management of people: kitchen staff, waiting staff, bar staff, all interacting with the customers.

What Carole recognised intuitively was that restaurant customers wanted, virtually demanded, a genuine, authentic service. Her role as '*la patronne*' enables her to supervise the business while mingling with and sharing stories with her customers. As one of her customers said to me, 'The food's pretty good at Moods, but what makes it really special is the way they treat you – it's not particularly flashy but you feel like they really want you to enjoy yourselves. Big restaurants get preoccupied with turning over volume and they don't really care.'

The tagline 'The Town's Best-Kept Secret' has a wonderful irony to it. If it is a secret then people want to know about it – after all a secret is something that you are not meant to share with others because then it becomes public property! Word-of-mouth referrals were the secret of their success – people being delighted to spread the word because sharing the secret gave you increased credibility (an unsophisticated but effective form of viral marketing).

Could a chain of restaurants capture Carole's formula and reproduce it across the country? Well they could run such a business but the process of cloning it would lose the essence of this small family concern – it might make the money but it just wouldn't be the same!

How do you differ from your competitors?

As a consequence of understanding how you differ, you can then focus your communications on what makes you different. Remember that if you are the same as your competition, then why should clients bother to buy from you?

Thought

Most people spend just about their entire life in one industry. They know everything there is to know about how their industry behaves, who the key players are, the recognised 'best' ways of buying/selling/running a business.

Assumption is laid on assumption after assumption about the right way to do things. And pretty much everyone else in the industry carries the same set of values. To gain some kind of advantage over the others, study and identify the fundamental principles that drive other industries. An approach that is common in one industry may be totally groundbreaking if applied to your industry.

- For instance, Federal Express applied the banking-system idea of the 'hub and spoke' to overnight delivery (this is the system where regional branches report to regional 'head' offices, which, in turn, report to the main head office).

- For instance, the roll-on deodorant was created after examination of a ballpoint pen.

ACTION POINT: Compare and contrast

Step 1
Randomly pick an industry unrelated to the one that you are working in.

Step 2
Write a list of ten things that the industry does better than yours (and say why) – perhaps use a contact in that industry to help you.

Step 3
Write a list of ten things *your* industry does better (and say why).

Step 4
Select four items from the list of ten things that the industry does better than yours (Step 2). Write down a list of twenty ways that you could apply *each* of those concepts to your industry.

Step 5
Evaluate your final list of eighty ideas – select five ideas that stand out as concepts worthy of pursuing. Develop these ideas and consider their feasibility.

ACTION POINT: Positioning the business

Establishing the business's position is a three-part process.

Step 1
List your competitors and list which customers or customer segments each competitor is aimed at.

Step 2
Write down your niche.

Step 3
Establish your position. The full brand-positioning exercise is described in the Seven-Point *Customer is King* Plan in Chapter 17.

Having attempted the positioning exercise, you can use the results to create or develop your brand-positioning statement, a simple one-page summary of the key elements that make up your brand personality and your brand proposition. This 'worksheet' helps your thinking about what attributes your brand should be carrying. The thinking about the issues is probably more important than the final output. The process considers establishing what you are and what you are not. It helps to define what you want your brand to represent.

Your brand-positioning statement should consider the following. There is a blank one to fill in for your business.

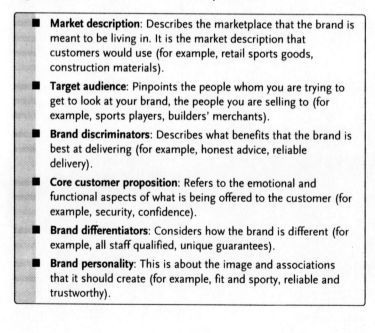

- **Market description**: Describes the marketplace that the brand is meant to be living in. It is the market description that customers would use (for example, retail sports goods, construction materials).

- **Target audience**: Pinpoints the people whom you are trying to get to look at your brand, the people you are selling to (for example, sports players, builders' merchants).

- **Brand discriminators**: Describes what benefits that the brand is best at delivering (for example, honest advice, reliable delivery).

- **Core customer proposition**: Refers to the emotional and functional aspects of what is being offered to the customer (for example, security, confidence).

- **Brand differentiators**: Considers how the brand is different (for example, all staff qualified, unique guarantees).

- **Brand personality**: This is about the image and associations that it should create (for example, fit and sporty, reliable and trustworthy).

Brand-positioning statement (BPS)

Market description:

Target audience:

Brand discriminators:

Core customer proposition:

Brand differentiator:

Brand personality:

Summary

If you can crack the brand positioning (in your customers' eyes) then you will know how best to communicate (in every sense) with your customers (existing and potential).

15: Creating a Customer Culture – a Thirteen-Point Plan

The 'building relationships' mantra is all too familiar to anyone who reads even a little about business. Over the past few years the gurus have drummed into us the value of developing long-term, loyal relationships with our customers (whatever all that means!).

- Why customers quit, what we can do.
- Benefits of a customer-initiative programme.
- How to keep customers for life – prove you care.

The 'bought-in' customers buy more and refer more, help us develop the next generation of products and services, and they even help us keep our advertising costs in check. All the up-tempo marketing hype certainly seems to have hit the mark. We all know what the reply is when we cry out the challenge, 'What is it that every so-called modern company wants right now?'

Question
Are your customers (people outside your organisation who buy things from you) the only people you should be building long-term relationships with?

Answer
No. The relationship strategy applies externally as well as internally.

Question
What if you were to take the concept of *customer* care and extend it outwards to your suppliers?

Answer

Your suppliers provide you with goods and services to which you usually add value and pass along to a customer (internal or external). If you began thinking of your supplier as your business partner, one with whom you share your dreams and visions of the future, one with whom you could achieve an ongoing, profitable relationship, you could be doing your customers a valuable service.

Score yourself

In your opinion, how well do you look after the customer? What score would you give yourself between one and ten? What score would your *customers* give *you*? Why don't you ask them?

Question

What if you were to take the concept of *customer* care and extend it inwards towards your employees?

Answer

The other group of people who can help you to achieve your goals and achieve your potential are the very people who work for you. Your employees, your staff, your associates, your workers, your colleagues – whatever you call them! In reality, these people are also your customers, your *internal* customers.

In the old, industrial model of businesses, employees served bosses, not customers. In today's apparently customer-driven marketplace, that has to change. The customer demands prompt and on-the-spot decisions, especially when they have a problem. The worker serves the customer, not the boss. This changes everything.

When you want the people who work for you to provide a level of care to customers that fosters long-term relationships, you have to provide a level of care for them (your people) that inspires, by example, trust, respect, open and honest communication and appreciation. Customers can tell when someone has a genuine interest in them and their wellbeing.

Care comes from caring. If you want to create value in the marketplace, create value first in the workplace.

Score yourself

How well do you look after your people? In your opinion what score would you give yourself between one and ten? What score would your *people* give *you*? Why don't you ask them?

Fact

If you treat your staff badly then you are sending them a message about how you expect them to treat others.

Opinion

If you treat your staff, your *internal* customers, properly, then the chances are that *they* will treat your *external* customers with just a bit more decency and respect.

Fact

Companies lose customers because they go elsewhere. And the reason they go elsewhere is that the people who serve them are indifferent to their needs.

So . . .

Do something about it! Hire people who want to give excellent customer service.

Fact

Actions speak louder than words.

Practice, not mere theory

A whole industry has been created around the softer side of the business, the people issues. The reality, for me, is not so much in well-meaning theory and the philosophy of people management. No, what matters is what you actually *do*!

Facts

- A typical business will hear from only **4 per cent** of its dissatisfied customers — the other 96 per cent will just quietly go away, 91 per cent never coming back.
- A typical dissatisfied customer will tell **eight to ten people** about his or her problem. One in five will tell twenty!

- **Seven out of ten** complaining customers will do business with you again if you resolve the complaint in their favour.
- You will probably **spend six times more** to attract new customers than you will to keep old ones.

Question
What is it that every so-called modern company wants right now?

Answer
'What we want,' we can imagine the reply to be from the typical business manager, 'are customers and employees who are loyal and excited by what we do. What we want to see is a commitment and a pride that shines through in everything we do. We want the phone lines jammed and the corridors awash with customers desperately wanting to do business with *us*!'

The reality is somewhat different. Yes, most companies have a few employees who do love their job and their customers and take real pride in their work. But, to be honest, just how many? Twenty per cent, ten per cent or fewer? Most still leave their brains in the staff car parks when they come to work. Pretty sad, really.

The '20:60:20 Rule of Staff Development' kicks in with a vengeance: generally, the top 20 per cent will be with you; 60 per cent will follow the top 20 per cent (eventually); and 20 per cent will never want to be moved.

It's one thing having a few of the fine people, the exemplars, in your organisation but how do you get to have more of them? Can you make more of your people care? Or do you have to employ new people?

The answer to these questions is pretty much stating the obvious: if you want your people to care about your customers then you have to set in motion a programme that proves that you care about your people.

Create a place where staff feel valued and encouraged and then your people will pass on their enthusiasm for the business to your customers. We already know about this, but we aren't very good at doing it!

Why customers quit

Research abounds to tell us why most customers quit. Companies lose customers in a variety of ways, and yet, according to M LeBoeuf, a staggering 68 per cent quit because of an attitude of indifference towards the customer! They believe we don't care about them:

- 1% die
- 3% move away
- 4% are natural floaters
- 5% move on recommendation
- 9% find somewhere cheaper
- 10% are chronic complainers
- 14% are dissatisfied
- 68% go elsewhere because the people who serve them are indifferent to their needs; they just don't care

Meanwhile the average company has to spend six times more to attract one new sale than to get a sale from an existing client.

What can we do?

You must design a programme (possibly involving training or consultancy interventions) so that your customers get an experience (from your staff) that makes them believe that you do care about them. Let's call this the *Customer-Initiative Programme*.

STEP 1

Create a workplace where all this naturally happens – where your people, your *internal* customers, are treated as well as you would expect them to treat your *external* customers. Lead by example.

STEP 2

Refocus the organisation's very purpose – putting the customer at the centre of the organisation changes how you do everything. Can you afford not to?

In your customer-initiative programme, you and your staff need to ask the following:

- Why do customers buy the product at all?
- Why do they buy it from you?
- How are you different from the competition?
- How will the customer benefit from this difference?
- What problem are you solving?
- What service levels do you expect to deliver?
- What service levels do the customers get?
- What are the minimum acceptable service standards?
- Do you understand and do you give basic courtesy?

Benefits of a customer-initiative programme

Focusing on the customer will improve business performance because your organisation will be better able to give the customer what they really want! Simple, basic techniques are required: for example, using existing information, or deciding which customers you want and then customising the service to fit their particular needs.

The discipline of putting the customer first brings with it systematic planning, prioritising, and measuring effectiveness, all of which help business performance. Focusing on customer needs changes the whole outlook of the business as it reviews all its functions in a new light.

By focusing on these needs, you are able to establish a competitive advantage as your people concentrate on what is really required of them by the customer!

Customer care (a.k.a. relationship marketing and customer excellence/loyalty/intimacy) can become the central business function, which increases the firm's competitiveness. Staff may well need to change in order to adopt the new philosophy, thus creating a sense of purpose about the organisation.

Strive constantly to increase the value that customers receive.

Serving the customer – questions to ask yourself

Companies endlessly claim to be in the business of customer service. How many actually take the time to find out what customer service really means? Nine times out of ten the service specification is defined not by the customer but by the service provider.

As part of the intervention you must ask the following of everyone in the organisation:

- What does your brand represent?
- What do your customers expect from you?
- How do they expect to be treated?
- How far do you exceed their expectations?
- What do you do when you fail to meet these expectations?
- Are your processes, systems and front-line people set up to give the sort of service that the 'promise' suggests?

How to keep customers for life

Any initiative to put the customers first must include the following:

- **Reward** them – make it feel good to do business with you; let them know what great service they are getting.
- **Forget** about selling – people love to buy; they hate to be sold at!
- **Remember** that people only buy good feelings and solutions to problems.
- **Keep asking** 'What's the unmet need?', 'How are we doing?', 'How can we do better?'

We are talking about shifting the way you work, about moving away from a focus on transactions and towards becoming a business built on relationships. All this takes persistence and passion!

At the risk of sounding trite, 'start with the end in mind' and prioritise accordingly – the journey to business success can be rewarding and exciting for everyone involved. Customer focus is not 'just another initiative': it is the only way forward!

You may wish to adopt a customer-service maxim

The trouble with the mantras and vision statements that the big businesses spend thousands developing is that they rapidly sound empty and vacuous. After that 'health warning', you may still wish to follow a customer-service maxim. Some typical ones run roughly along the following lines:

- 'Customers are our bosses.'
- 'Our customers pay the bills.'
- 'The customer is always right.'
- 'Customers are people, not numbers.'
- 'Customers are our best source of customers.'
- 'Customers R Us.'
- 'Customers do not depend on us: we depend on them.'
- 'Customers do not interrupt our work: they are the reason that we are here.'
- 'What customers value most are attention, dependability, promptness and competence.'

Summary

Perhaps the best way to sum up the points in this chapter is to present what its title promised: the Thirteen-Point Plan – a plan to prove you care.

1. Have a written document outlining your principles of customer service.
2. Establish systems that focus on service superiority.
3. Measure and reward.
4. Passion for the value of excellent service must run through every part of the business.
5. Be genuinely committed to being better than anyone else in the industry.
6. Be sure you all pay close attention to the customer.
7. Ask questions of the customer and *listen* to the answers.
8. Stay in touch with customers.

9. Be alert to trends.
10. Share information with the front line.
11. Recognise the human as well as the business relationship.
12. Invest in systems that make your whole business sound friendly.
13. Remember: what customers value most are attention, dependability, promptness and competence (Jay Levinson).

16: A Game of Twenty Questions

Pick one or two or ten of the following questions and use them provocatively to stimulate thought (and even a little conflict) – get the blood going. Remember, a 'twenty-first-century mind' questions old assumptions and models and looks for ways continuously to improve.

■ Provocative questions for you to consider about your business.

The questions

1. Is the level of trust in your organisation high or low?
2. How do you help individuals cultivate a feeling of pride in their work?
3. When you delegate responsibility, do you also delegate authority along with it?
4. Do employees get involved in discussions about things that will affect their future?
5. Knowing that creativity and innovation are critical to your future, is training and development an important part of your strategic plan?
6. What methods do you use to show your people that you appreciate them and their work?
7. What mechanisms are in place to reward the kinds of customer-caring behaviour you want to see repeated?
8. Do employees really believe that open and honest communication on their part will not damage their careers?
9. What are you doing to encourage people constantly to think 'continuous improvement'?
10. What are the five most important values in your organisa-

tion? How do your management and staff demonstrate them every day?

11. On a scale of one to ten, how much real, honest-to-goodness fun are people having in your organisation?

12. If you ask your employees to take risks, are you wholeheartedly accepting their failures (so-called 'learning experiences') as well as their successes?

13. Do you really believe your employees are capable of being fully empowered? If not, what's missing? Do you want them empowered?

14. Are there negative consequences when someone makes the decision to please the customer rather than please the boss?

15. Do your corporate definitions of success include the non-monetary things such as job satisfaction and individual growth? How do you measure it?

16. And here is one more question to upset your next management meeting: Have you recently surveyed the staff to find out how they really feel about working with you and whether or not they really have what they need to take 'exquisite' care of the customers?

Remember, if you want to create more value in the marketplace, you need to create more value in the workplace. Go to it. Here are three more questions for good measure:

17. Just how special does it feel to be one of your customers?

18. As a business, do you treat customers the same as other suppliers do? Or better then other suppliers? Or do you provide customers with a 'wow!' experience?

19. How many customers see you as 'head and shoulders' above the competition?

And you can choose Question 20 for yourself!

PART TWO

17: The Seven-Point *Customer is King* Plan

The Seven-Point Customer is King *Plan is a step-by-step process for getting your business to see itself through your customers' eyes and to start to make sure that you can design a business that delivers on its promise and delights its customers – this is a systematic way to develop your business.*

The seven points of the *Customer is King* plan are these:

1. Redefine your business as a problem solver.
2. Understand the real scope of your business.
3. Get under each customer's skin!
4. Stand out in order to be outstanding.
5. Develop a strategy to define your position.
6. Calculate just how much a customer is worth to you.
7. Select your weapons.

I will explain what I mean by each of these in the following chapters.

The seven-point plan has been worked through by businesses, both big and small, across the world. It is used for several reasons. Sometimes it is used to clarify direction, almost as part of a team-building activity, to remind the team of what they are trying to do. Sometimes it is used to develop a PR and branding strategy, or even to help to define the vision and mission of the business.

There are a number of different ways that it can be applied to the business. For example:

- as a tool to stimulate and motivate the sales team
- as a tool to focus on improving profitability
- as a tool to help the owner-manager to understand how to grow the business

- as a tool to ensure that the business is being totally focused on what really matters
- as a PR tool to invite customers and suppliers to start dialogue

The key issue is that the plan must be applied to the business. It must add value to the bottom line; it must be used as a springboard to *improve* your business. It is a powerful and far-reaching tool that will energise and stimulate your organisation and your people to grow the business.

Bad questions get bad answers. Great questions demand great answers. For instance, 'Can we do better?' is a bad question because it is too vague and doesn't challenge the person being asked. 'Can you think of three ways that you could increase turnover without spending a penny?' is a great question because it engages the listener.

The seven-point plan is all about great questions. For instance:

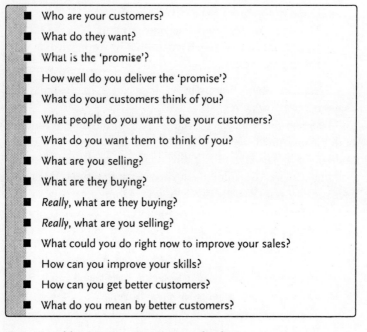

- Who are your customers?
- What do they want?
- What is the 'promise'?
- How well do you deliver the 'promise'?
- What do your customers think of you?
- What people do you want to be your customers?
- What do you want them to think of you?
- What are you selling?
- What are they buying?
- *Really*, what are they buying?
- *Really*, what are you selling?
- What could you do right now to improve your sales?
- How can you improve your skills?
- How can you get better customers?
- What do you mean by better customers?

Can you add your own questions to this list?

Summary

The Seven-Point *Customer is King* Plan is a systematic process for fine-tuning and/or establishing what business sales you will get from which customers, against whom and how.

18: The Seven-Point *Customer is King* Plan – 1: Redefine Your Business as a Problem Solver

Most businesses see themselves as a producer. When company owners or managers introduce themselves, they say things like, 'We're a pizza restaurant; we make pizzas' or 'We're a video production company; we make videos.' This is a naïve position to adopt, because you are so much more than just a maker of pizzas, or just a maker of videos!

> ■ Become problem-seeking and problem-solving.

Many of the so-called 'new economy' businesses are preoccupied with branding. To be more accurate, they are preoccupied with putting out a message about themselves. They confuse the message with the messenger!

Bigger companies get intoxicated with the idea of selling the 'courageous message' of the brand (the attitude, 'Just do it', 'The real thing') rather than the product itself. There is a belief in the larger corporations that branding provides the opportunity for seemingly limitless growth; the brand can be attached to almost any product. Look at the exponential growth in the range of products and services attached to a brand name such as Nike. For most of us, such a position is unrealistic.

To get to the heart of what your business does, you need to redefine yourself.

What *real* problems are you solving?

Sometimes you need to change how you see yourself, change the perception that you are using to look at the world. To understand the customer experience and to take advantage of it, redefine yourself as a problem solver!

The word 'redefine' like those well-known words such as 're-engineering' and 're-creating', smacks of theory rather than action. What I mean by 'redefine' is simply that you need to take on a different mindset in order to change how you see your business and your customers.

If you put yourself in the role of 'problem solver' for your clients, you start to look for problems to solve. Rather than look for sales, you look for the problems that the client is facing. However, when you focus on the customers' problems, a number of things happen:

- ■ You start to see things through the customer's eyes.
- ■ You start to see the real issues that the customer faces.
- ■ You are able to have more empathy as you try to see what help the client might need.
- ■ You develop a stronger relationship because you are not constantly wearing your 'sales hat'.
- ■ You are developing long-term rather than short-term relationships.

By running your business as if it were a problem solver, suddenly you have a significant role to play for the customer. Your role is that of one who figures out what your customers are trying to do and helps them to do it. When you wear this different pair of spectacles, the world takes on a different shape.

Case study: The HotHouse Pizza Restaurant

What problem are they solving? Customers want a tasty, hot meal delivered to their table, quickly and courteously. They may be having a meal in their lunch hour or celebrating their child's tenth birthday. Either way, the restaurant needs to understand what the customer really wants and, more importantly, what the customer *doesn't* want.

But the story doesn't end here. All pizza houses will claim to understand their customers' needs (all those wonderful empty slogans that proclaim that the customer is king). All pizza houses try to keep their customers happy. But is that it? I think that this is just the beginning.

HotHouse's Vic Talbot went on to create a series of special dinner 'packages' – early and late meals for theatre- and filmgoers, a party package for special birthdays, an outside-catering package, reservations by email, a special email offering discounts on quiet nights ('Visit us tonight and we'll give you a twenty per cent discount'). These ideas all came from a special meet-the-chefs evening when customers were invited to come along and see behind the scenes and offer suggestions and advice on how the HotHouse service could be improved.

What else could they have done? What do you think the customers thought about what was going on? If you took Vic out for a drink, what things would you be suggesting that he try? And what would Vic say to you if he saw behind the scenes at your business?

Let us examine another case.

Case study: BLT Video Productions

What problem are they solving? Clients have fundamental communication needs. Corporate videos act as 'advertorial' to promote a company; TV commercials and pop videos must deliver to a specific, yet creative, brief. Clients don't usually know exactly what they want; nor do they know what is possible within a given budget.

'The role of the production company isn't simply to make a video,' says BLT's Toby Michael. 'The role can extend so much further – the more that the client feels part of the decision-making process and understands the options that are available, the more that they will understand and appreciate what has been done. Here, educating the client may be a key to helping the client to make the right decisions. BLT produced a video [in their downtime] showing what is possible within different budgets – followed by a collation of some of their best pieces of work – a piece of dynamite in terms of creating effective sales opportunities.'

Even this may be too lightweight an approach. What else could they be doing at BLT? Do you think that they have done enough? The ability to really identify what the real problem is would enable you to provide a real solution.

So what?

Part of being a problem solver is recognising that your job is to help the customer. You are their helper. You help them to enjoy their meal, or you help them to run a better business, or you help them to have a relaxing weekend. Think of your last disappointed customer. How could you have done a better job of helping?

David Hall, author of *Doing the Business* (also published in this series), refers to this characteristic as 'problem-seeking/problem-solving' for customers. Successful companies stay close to their customers and work in partnership – they will take on their customers' problems as their own problems. They seek problems for the present and potential/future customers and they seek out and look for solutions – as a result they can become friends for life.

ACTION POINT: Searching questions

Answer the following for your business:

- Why do people come to your business?
- Why do people buy your product/service?
- Why do they buy it from you?
- What problems do they have that you are trying to solve?
- What would their ideal solution be? (What should they be saying, thinking and doing as a result of visiting your business?)
- What is *your* ideal solution? (What should they be saying, thinking and doing as a result of visiting your business?)
- For a moment, forget about the need to make a sale. If you use the mindset of a problem solver, what else could you be doing to make life easier for your customer?

ACTION POINT: Problem-solving exercise

1. Draw up a list of ten clients.
2. For each client, write down three problems that they are currently facing; these do not necessarily need to be problems with what you sell to them.
3. Now, look for solutions. At the least, this enables you to have a more far-reaching conversation with the client; it shows that you are really thinking about them and also demonstrates your ability 'to help' in its broadest sense. This is a powerful way to develop your relationship with clients.
4. Go to each of the ten clients and share your ideas and thoughts with them.

Summary

Become problem-seeking and problem-solving – the greatest compliment is when a customer starts to see you as a resource rather than a product salesperson, and asks you to help them sort something out. Work hard to get as close to your customers as they will allow you!

What business are you in? What's your product, and what are its benefits?

> ■ Understand the scope and depth of how you can help.

Most of us repeatedly undersell ourselves. As well as underselling ourselves, we often misunderstand how we are perceived: there is a gap between what *we* think we do and what the *customer* sees. In a business, such a gap results in dissatisfied customers and poor performance.

I was at a seminar recently and a delegate approached me and insisted I tell him why his business was not working. First, I asked him to explain his business to me, and he launched into a ten-minute monologue on the differences between full-bandwidth, multidigital, infrared sensors and the standard, analogue, relay-oriented, transistorised, bimodular systems that they were competing with.

To be quite frank, I didn't have a clue what he was talking about. He went on and on about how this new idea could make him a millionaire ten times over and yet he wanted to know why no one would buy from him.

I asked him how he thought he came across when he met people and he said, and I quote, 'People really enjoy listening to me tell them about my product; I know that because people never interrupt me. And that's why I have the potential to be such a great salesman.'

At this point I was called away but my point is simple. This man was obsessed with the *features* of his product but wasn't interested in (or wasn't able to see) *how well he came across*. As I left, his final point to me was, 'You do realise that the problem with my business isn't me, but the customers – they just don't recognise an opportunity when they see one.' This man did not seem to make too much effort to understand what the customer wanted or needed from the relationship.

So . . .

> ■ Do you ever get carried away with the features of your product and forget that the customer may not be on the same wavelength as you?
>
> ■ Do you ask enough questions of your customers?
>
> ■ Do you really listen to your customers and what they want?

What is the point?

If you have too narrow a vision of what you offer to customers, then you will undersell yourself; you will miss opportunities to develop the relationship. If, on the other hand, you understand the scope and depth of how you can help, then you will discover new opportunities to work with and help your customer.

Case study: Yummy and scrummy!

Liam Andrew set up Yum-Scrums delicatessen after many years in the banking industry. Located in an out-of-town location, Liam was quick to recognise that his customers wanted new taste experiences. He imported a French bread oven and imported frozen French bread dough so that he was the first business in town to make what tasted like proper French bread.

Further discussions with local businesses identified a further opportunity – offices and workplaces on the outskirts of town had poor access to lunchtime food. Liam bought a wonderful old Morris Minor van, painted it up and started a delivery service to all the major out-of-town employers. This proved to be a huge success and, subsequently, Liam invested in several more vans to keep pace with demand.

His staff now start work at 3 a.m. to make delicious sandwiches and snacks for the delivery service.

What else could Liam have done? What services would you like your local equivalent of Yum-Scrums to provide? Could you describe your ideal delicatessen – if Liam knew what you, a potential customer, thought then couldn't he possibly take on some of those ideas?

Case study: Terridge's ironmongers

For ten years, Terridge's has performed moderately well as a small local ironmonger selling all types of product for do-it-yourself and household work.

Don Terridge employed seven people and had a regular local trade. The business had a little monopoly, because it was the only shop of its kind in town. Then a large chain of DIY warehouses set up nearby, Terridge's became deserted as most of Don's so-called loyal customers were lured towards the heavily advertised special offers at the new shop.

Don knew that the warehouse was no cheaper on a product-by-product basis. However he felt unable to defend himself from this attack on his livelihood. He was even talking about closing down.

Don had spent the last few years protected from the harsh realities of business. The business had pottered along without really trying too hard. Turnover had been adequate for Don to maintain a comfortable lifestyle. Fortunately, the DIY superstore shocked Don into action.

A conversation I had with Don turned the whole situation to his advantage. Although he hadn't realised it, Don had unparalleled product information, but it was all in his head.

He knew *exactly* why people visit a shop like his: they had problems. For instance, they want to fix a mirror to a wall, or they want to get rid of an infestation of ants, or they are about to undertake a big project in the garden. And, usually, the customer isn't quite sure how to do the job. More than anything else, the customer needs some guidance and assurance about the best way to tackle the job.

There was hardly a job that Don and his staff hadn't done around the house and garden. They had used all their own products and knew exactly how they performed. More than that, they knew the tricks of the trade, the shortcuts to make the work easier.

The power formula that the warehouse couldn't compete with was the friendly yet encyclopedic knowledge that Terridge's willingly and genuinely shared with its customers.

Don made all his staff spend as much time as possible with each customer to understand fully what they were trying to do. Don says, 'I've trained all my staff to always ask customers what they're trying do before selling them any product. This way we can give them what they need (rather than what they want) and we can give them some advice that usually saves them money and also increases the chance of them doing a decent job! And all this increases the chances of them coming back as well.'

Don Terridge is the first to admit that he isn't exactly a 'modern' businessman. What other opportunities could Don have considered? What about an Internet presence, and, if so, why? Should he consider equipment hire or getting involved in doing general building work?

The moral of the story is: don't be too quick to use a self-limiting definition of what you do. Very often there are countless opportunities that just go missing. Always think about expanding the boundaries of your definition.

ACTION POINT: What's new?

For your business, write down a list of ten items for each of the following:

 ■ ten products/services that are almost identical to your existing offerings

- ten products/services that are an extension of your existing offerings
- ten products/services that are a new departure from your existing offerings
- ten markets/customers that are almost identical to your existing markets/customers
- ten markets/customers that are an extension of your existing markets/customers
- ten markets/customers that are a new departure from your existing markets/customers

Have you come up with any possible new products worth considering?

Hmm . . . something to think about
What's your power formula that your competitors cannot compete with?

Summary

Expand the limits of how you define your business. Consider how you could expand into new or different product/service line and/or new or different markets. Think laterally.

Consider the advantages and disadvantages of becoming broader in your scope or becoming narrower/deeper in your scope.

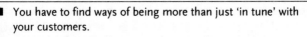

20: The Seven-Point *Customer is King* Plan – 3: Get Under Each Customer's Skin!

Get under the skin of every customer. It's the way to find out how they tick.

- You have to find ways of being more than just 'in tune' with your customers.
- The customer-experience cycle.

Here are some more crunch questions:

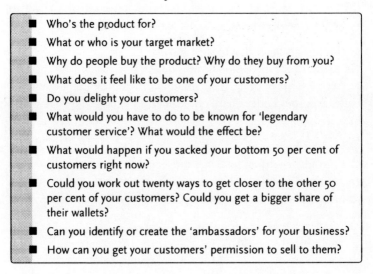

- Who's the product for?
- What or who is your target market?
- Why do people buy the product? Why do they buy from you?
- What does it feel like to be one of your customers?
- Do you delight your customers?
- What would you have to do to be known for 'legendary customer service'? What would the effect be?
- What would happen if you sacked your bottom 50 per cent of customers right now?
- Could you work out twenty ways to get closer to the other 50 per cent of your customers? Could you get a bigger share of their wallets?
- Can you identify or create the 'ambassadors' for your business?
- How can you get your customers' permission to sell to them?

Getting under the skin of your customer is no easy task. Nearly every large business (with its big budgets) is trying to find out what makes its customers tick. Endless customer surveys by market-research companies try to figure out how to sell more product to the poor unsuspecting (?) customers. Are there ways that you can get this valuable information without using a big budget?

While fast-moving consumer goods and global brands try to establish common major themes that will catch the majority – the 'average' consumer – the field is open for those businesses pursuing the smaller, more specific markets, the niches. This is where the smaller business, with its ability to move quickly and nimbly, can find more than enough customers to satisfy its own business needs.

So, if you are in the fortunate position where you have actually established exactly who it is you wish to sell to, what next to understand is what your customers want. There are various options, some traditional, some more innovative. Here are just eight of them.

1. Customer focus groups
Take a dozen existing (or prospective, or past) customers and ask them what they think about the product/service, ask them about the competition and ask them what your business should do to make the customer want to do more business with you.

2. Net survey via a discussion forum
Go to one of the discussion forums on the Internet and ask the subscribers what they think. You could ask them to fill in a questionnaire. You could offer them a sweetener: a discount, say, or a token of your appreciation.

3. Student help
Get a student to do a so-called university project – this guise will enable them to write and speak to your competitors and customers to find out what they think of you and how you could improve your service.

4. Invite them to dinner
Run a private dinner/event for a select group of customers – opin-

ion formers/leaders – in a private dining room. Make them feel that the dinner is exclusive. Make them feel like VIPs and that their opinions/reactions are valued.

Have a specific theme that you wish to talk about, or tell them about the launch of a new product or piece of research, and make them feel privileged by giving them an exclusive preview. After the meal and the networking, you can start subtly to pick their brains. For example, 3i, the venture-capital company, run boardroom briefings and dinners to lobby or measure reactions to their latest research or initiative – I am delighted to be invited, I feel flattered and benefit from rubbing shoulders with other guests; 3i benefit from lobbying us and hearing our views.

5. Write articles

While researching an article for a trade paper you can interview your customers and feature their comments. In the interview, you can explore how and why they buy your product. They will feel flattered that you have asked for their opinion. They will feel flattered when they see their name in print. They will see you as more than just a supplier. You will gain invaluable market/customer knowledge, which you can share in the article.

You could use the article to show what the leading-edge suppliers (i.e. you) are doing. As a result, you may even get invited to give presentations at conferences as you establish a reputation as a key player in the industry.

6. Conference or a seminar

This is another opportunity to invite your customers to a forum where you can meet them and share and discuss things. A good theme might be future-based to get people thinking about how their needs might change in the future.

For example, a theme based on the future of the print industry may look at how to use 'the latest technology' to increase your profits.

7. Special suppliers' seminars

The *Financial Times* runs occasional lunches to allow their far-flung contributors to come 'up to the Smoke' and compare notes while being updated on the latest things happening at the paper.

8. Customer days

One of the best of these that I went to was run by the Coventry print company Emerson Press, who put on curry-and-lager lunches at their print works. At 2 p.m. a klaxon sounds and the printing machinery begins to run. Customers love to see something actually being made in front of their eyes; questions start to flow and relationships are built as customers realise that print is not simply a commodity bought on price but a skilled job that requires a care and an understanding on the part of the printer to give you, the customer, what you want.

Get under your customer's skin

Somehow you've got to find ways of being more than just in tune with your customers. To get ahead of your competitors you need to understand what it is that your customers want and to demonstrate that you *understand* what they want and need, and be able to do it better than your competitors.

The saying 'Get under each customer's skin' has different implications depending on where you place the emphasis. Let's take the different ways that you can say it:

- '*Get* under each customer's skin' – it is up to you to make the effort to ask questions and make the effort.

- 'Get *under* each customer's skin' – try to imagine what it feels like to be a customer; dig deep; try being one of your customers. What does it actually feel like and what else do you think about?

- 'Get under *each* customer's skin' – do you see all customers as the same or do you treat them as individuals? Do you customise your product enough for the customer or do you pretend to? Does it matter whether you deliver a standard or bespoke product? What would be the benefits of becoming more or less bespoke (from the customer's point of view)? What would be the benefits of focusing on each individual rather than seeing them as a mass of people with the same basic requirements?

■ 'Get under each *customer's* skin' – think of existing customers and old customers and potential customers and people who no longer wish to do business with you. All of these people can be potential sources for creating additional products and services.

■ 'Get under each customer's *skin*' – on the one hand, skin is tactile so reach out and touch these people. The verb 'to skin' is about stripping back the skin – look inside, under the surface, to see what these people might want and what they really think and feel.

ACTION POINT: How can we help you?

Jot down the names of your ten best customers. Then contact each one – first by phone and then by follow-up letter – and simply tell them that you want them to know how much you appreciate the business they've done with you and how you respect their opinion.

Tell them that you are trying to grow the business and wondering whether they could help you be answering a few questions. You might wish to invite them out to eat with you. The questions that you want answers to include:

■ What do you really like about the way we do business?

■ What drives you mad about the way we do business?

■ If you ran my business, what five changes would you make and why?

■ What opportunities am I missing?

■ If we are going to grow the business, what aspects must we keep and what must we lose?

■ What could we do that would make you want to buy more from us?

■ What do you think our other customers think about us?

■ Whom do you see as our main competitors and how are they better or worse than we are?

This exercise will give you plenty to think about.

The customer experience cycle

A lot of businesses find the concept of the 'customer experience cycle' useful when they are trying to get a handle on what their customers go through. The cycle makes the assumption that each customer goes through a three-stage process. In terms of our product/service:

- Step One: They get it.
- Step Two: They use it.
- Step Three: They fix it.

In each stage of this cycle we can add to our own understanding of the customer by seeking to grasp and solve the problems that the customer faces. At each stage, there are different things going on for the customer.

Step One
The customer gets it – for instance, buying a lawnmower: the salesperson should be interested in what it is wanted for (for what it is provided: lawn cutting) and why it is wanted (the result: a tidy lawn).

Step Two
They use it – how easy is it to use and what difficulties or add-ons might there be?

Step Three
They fix it – with ownership come issues of maintenance and servicing. How easy or difficult does the customer find it to maintain the machine?

Can you apply the customer experience cycle to your business? Can you think of ways that you could make things better for the customer? Can you see new opportunities that could be exploited by you or a colleague or a competitor?

Gather together your customer-facing people. Brainstorm for, say, fifteen minutes. Take each stage of the cycle and explore how you can do better. Seek new, different or innovative ways of increasing or improving the customer experience.

Below is a sample of the ideas generated at Minniver magazine publishers.

Step One: They get it

- At the post office? By mail order? With their milk? When they get their car serviced? Free in hotel rooms? By lifetime subscription? With membership of a club?
- Do the covers turn on the 'right people' and make them want to buy it?
- Should there be a parallel site on the Internet?
- They get it in smaller parts/bigger parts?
- More materials that run over several issues?
- They help to write it and get more involved?
- Do they know about the 'next issue' in the next issue?
- Do we make it easy to buy the magazine?

Step Two: They use it

- A parallel discussion forum on the web?
- Better-quality paper?
- Different format? A4?
- Are we sure the content appeals to the right people? What do we mean by the right people?
- Should we create a club atmosphere? Should we create a club?
- A hardback version? Or spiral bound?
- More checklists or things to do?
- More hotlines?
- More community?

Step Three: They fix it

> - Could we create an automatic retrieval system – a way to get back to an old article (via the web)?
> - Could we offer every twelve issues as a volume for people who want to collect all editions or may have missed one edition at the newsstand?
> - Should we sell back issues at premium prices?
> - Should the magazine self-destruct?
> - Should it be so 'time-sensitive'?
> - What else should our readers get/have to deepen their relationship with each other (and with us)?
> - Should we have a password to join a club on the web where you can see back copies and get special offers?

The abbreviated notes from the brainstorming session reflect how the session went. It generated lots of new ideas about offering readers more than just a magazine. In fact the publishing company started to redefine itself. Because they had always referred to 'readers', they had narrowed their view on what they made and the service that they offered. Their particular audience actually felt underrepresented and saw the magazine as a conduit to audience-specific products and services.

Subscribers wanted the branding of the magazine to give them a sense of security when they bought products through its pages. In fact, they wanted to buy through the magazine's own small mail-order outlet. This realisation led to the discovery of the company's best growth opportunity.

Summary

The benefits of sincerely understanding what it feels like to be one of your customers will pay back many times over. Your customers will thank you and it will make your job and the jobs of all your people much easier and much more pleasurable. You will be able to focus your efforts on giving your customers what they really want.

21: The Seven-Point *Customer is King* Plan – 4: Stand Out in Order to be outstanding

Can you make yourself different from the rest? Can you position yourself against the rest?

- How to differentiate yourself from the rest.
- One way to deliver the difference is through the 'service experience'.

The theme that runs through this book is: If you are the same as the rest then why should customers bother to buy from you? Ignore it at your peril! In a world where competition seems to be everywhere, you need to separate yourself from the rest.

Fact
If you compete on price, only the customer will win – the company with the lowest prices (which means the biggest buying power) will get the business. This is no place for the timid.

So what?
If you try to be the same as the rest, a 'me-too' business, it is incredibly difficult to survive in the long run. After all, the only way you can differentiate yourself when several businesses are selling exactly the same product will be on price. And, if you differentiate yourself on price, then it becomes inevitable that you enter a price war – customers will chase the cheapest prices.

Those businesses with the biggest market share (and economies of scale) will be able command better prices from their suppliers. As a result, these competitors will be able to pass on those savings to customers while maintaining healthier profit margins than their competition (probably, you). You will end up cutting your profit margins, probably until you go out of business.

Definition
To differentiate is to set yourself apart, to be seen to be different (in the customer's eyes). One way is to make the customer feel in control.

Opinion or maybe even a fact!
You must differentiate yourself from the rest. It is this need to differentiate your business that leads to the concept of 'positioning'. More of this later – see page 154.

Fact
We now live in an 'experience' economy.

In today's world, the big-budget brands are often treated with suspicion. They now need to prove themselves. Old-world marketing tried to give different personalities to what were essentially similar products. Think of the weak wet stuff known as lager in the eighties. Nowadays, customers are inclined to think that, if a product looks, sounds, smells, feels and performs in roughly the same manner, then it probably is roughly the same. So somehow you must create that difference that separates you from all the other similar products.

Fact
Perception is reality (until proven otherwise).

Opinion or maybe even a fact!
Brand preference has always been a function of perception. People prefer the brand that they believe will give them what they want; marketing is usually a battle of perceptions more than a battle of products. In today's world you have to try much harder to create (and maintain) the perceived difference.

If you want to be more successful at creating and maintaining the perceived difference of your product, then the customer's experience should be made to be unique in tangible, physical ways. A corollary to this is that if your service is intangible then a powerful way of branding yourself is by creating tangible (and ideally memorable) experiences.

How do you do that, then?

One way to deliver the difference is through the 'service experience'. 'Doubting Thomas' consumers demand tangible differences in your product or service. These differences can be part of your media or retail strategy. But do not make claims that cannot be substantiated. There is a general shift away from style and towards substance. People no longer confuse the sizzle with the steak!

What does all this mean?

Be aware of the critical role that relationships have in the customer–supplier interactions. It is very 'now' to talk about customer relationships, but actually delivering on the promise of 'getting close to the customer' is something else. Big businesses endlessly try to get close to the customer, to become the customer's friend. Just look at the way that the large banks and retail chains portray themselves.

Smaller business can win hands down in terms of actually caring about and listening to the customer. (But, remember, with more modest training and advertising budgets, the smaller business also has the capacity to screw up – big time!)

Opinion

In a world where everyone copies each other, it takes a lot to keep your experience different. In our novelty culture, it takes even more effort to keep the customers' experience fresh and surprising. How is this to be done?

Two ways to add to experiences through communication

To heighten an experience there are two things that you can do: you can create expectations and/or you can 'condition' the experience.

To create expectations or heighten an experience can be fairly straightforward: one way is to tell the customer what to look for. For example, Wines2You include tasting notes with their wines containing such suggestions as 'notice the flavours of buttered toast, some say slightly burnt toast'. Suddenly, the client tunes into these flavours and probably passes on this titbit of information to friends when drinking the wine (to show off their new knowledge).

Another example is pop concerts, where there is often a build-up to the arrival of the star on stage: 'The Spice Girls will be on stage in thirty minutes.'

And then there's advertising that often conditions your experience: 'Notice how much fresher-smelling and cleaner-looking . . .' To condition the experience you need to add a creative idea. This adds to the experience, often in terms of romance or mystique. Wines2You tasting notes, for instance, go on to say how Wines2You's managing director, Keith, first met the owner of the vineyard early one scorching summer's morning in the northernmost part of Spain, celebrating the birth of his first child in one of the sixteenth-century caves at his smallholding. CD covers celebrate a musician's roots: '. . . brought up in the deep South in the depression of . . .' Or, 'Moussa comes from a long line of the kings of the kora, the traditional African instrument that dates back to the times of . . .'

Law 9 of The Immutable Laws of Customer-Focused Marketing – the First Law

You will find this law repeated when we list these laws later, but there is no harm in giving you a taster here. If you aren't Number One in your existing 'category' then create your own category, or be the first in customers' minds. A category might be local burger bars, marketing consultants, vets, precision engineers, or even structural engineers.

ACTION POINT: Delivering uniqueness

> ■ How could you 'add' to your business offering? Could you be nicer or smarter or faster or brighter or slower or what?

- How can you make it more special or even unique? What do your customers or suppliers comment on as the special thing that makes you different?

- How can you show off your individuality? Are there ways that you can display your uniqueness? Is there any one trait that you think your competitors might be jealous of? (Your brilliant attention to detail or your extraordinary industry knowledge or your ability to deliver within the hour, for instance?)

- In what way can you make your offering even a little different from the rest?

- What is it that everyone else does in a certain fashion but you could do better or differently?

The difference between 'differentiation' and 'positioning'

The difference between differentiation and positioning is, in my mind, a semantic difference – a fascinating dialogue can be had by the academics, but who cares!

Positioning is the process of distinguishing a brand from its competitors so that it becomes a preferred brand in defined segments of the market. Ries and Trout say:

Positioning starts with the product. A piece of merchandise, a service, a company, an institution, or even a person . . . But positioning is not what you do to a product. Positioning is what you do to the mind of the prospect. That is, you position the product in the mind of the prospect.

Differentiation is about how you choose to target your markets:

- Undifferentiated marketing ignores segments and attacks a whole market, aiming to satisfy the common needs of customers.

- Differentiated marketing operates in several segments/sections of the market and designs separate offers for each.

- Concentrated marketing aims for a large share in a few segments.

Summary

You must make yourself different from the rest. No business can profit without winning over the hearts and minds of its target customers – well, not for long. In a world where competition seems to be everywhere, you need to separate yourself from the rest.

22: The Seven-Point *Customer is King* Plan – 5: Develop a Strategy to Define Your Position

'Strategy' is one of the most overused words in business. Strategy is planning your business, while being aware of the business environment. If you plan the future without taking account of the environment in which you are trading then you really are gambling with the future of your business.

- Positioning your business in three steps.
- A brand-positioning statement.

'How can I go forward when I don't know which way I am facing? How can I go forward when I don't know which way to turn?' (John Lennon, 'How?', from *Imagine*, 1971).

A cool and calm analysis of your business environment will consider the following key factors that may influence how you should consider and plan your future. (See the chapters on strategy in *Kick-Start Your Business*.)

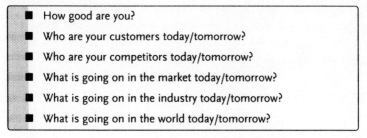

- How good are you?
- Who are your customers today/tomorrow?
- Who are your competitors today/tomorrow?
- What is going on in the market today/tomorrow?
- What is going on in the industry today/tomorrow?
- What is going on in the world today/tomorrow?

Once you have considered your business environment you can piece together your strategy for your business. In a logical format you can determine your strategy as follows:

> ■ What is your blue-skies vision for the business? What would success smell and taste like? What would the business be known for in, say, three years' time, if it were successful? This is, of course, a very 'touchy-feely' way to describe the business. You can then move on to . . .
>
> ■ What is your mission for the business? If you were to achieve your vision, what would the 'numbers' be? How many people would you employ? What would your turnover be? What would your profit margins be? Now you can move on to . . .
>
> ■ Your strategy, the way that you are going to achieve your vision and mission. How are you going to achieve your vision and mission? By being quicker? Or smarter? Or brighter? Or higher quality? Or more safety-conscious? Or more environmental? Will you be cheaper? Or more acquisitive? Or will you grow by organic growth?

Positioning

Positioning is at the heart of strategy formulation for your business. It is one of the hardest parts of 'reinventing' your business. For many businesspeople, it is relatively easy to understand what positioning is and how to do it. The difficulty comes in the execution, the doing bit.

'Positioning' is . . .

Positioning is all about understanding the map of where (and how and against whom) you are competing. Positioning is a difficult process. It is a creative, subjective process. Positioning helps you understand why you are different or points to how you could emphasise your difference. Positioning suggests a version of the territory; it is a map. But maps do not always reflect the reality that you see on the ground.

Doing 'positioning' in three steps

How do you differ from your competitors? As a consequence of understanding how you differ, you can then focus your actions and your communications on what makes you different. Remember that if you are the same as your competition, then why should clients bother to buy from you?

Establishing the business's position is a three-part process.

Step 1

List your competitors and list which customers or customer segments each competitor is aimed at.

Draw up a list of your key competitors. Next to each competitor, list the customers or target customer segments that the competitor focuses on. What will emerge is that different competitors are focusing on different niches or subsectors of the market.

Step 2

Write down your niche. In other words, which customers or customer segment are you aimed at?

Be specific about whom you aim your business activities at. Consider your key competitors for those customers.

Often we work so hard to get the product out of the factory gate that we forget to remind ourselves exactly what we are trying to do. More importantly, we need to have a thorough understanding of the competitive environment that we are competing in.

Step 3

Establish your position. Establishing your position is a very unstructured process, be warned. It helps you to understand your competitive environment. However, just because it is so ill-defined, it doesn't mean that you shouldn't do it.

The position is mapped out in what is called a brand-positioning matrix. Essentially, it is a box. The box has two different axes that allow you to map out the competing businesses according to how they score on the respective axes.

Case study:

Jim McPherson's training business, MCP, struggled to establish some kind of 'uniqueness' in its early days. All training businesses, small or large, claim to offer unique, bespoke solutions tailored to the client's needs, working in partnership with the client (remember Jim's visit to the Annual Training Providers' Conference in Chapter 8?).

In fact, it is almost impossible to differentiate the competition because everyone makes the same promises. So the task was to find a way to separate the business from the similar-sounding competitors.

After using the Same/Better/'Wow!' Index, Jim worked on positioning – this method would help him to see the differences between him and his competitors in terms of the overall offering to customers.

After several hours of trying out different combinations of headings for the axes, Jim's management team finally found a set of headings that would separate themselves out from the rest. The headings chosen were

- type of output/work done
- style of dealing with clients

Competitors
Big training companies
Business schools
Government/business support agencies
Independent freelance trainers

Axis 1: type of output:
A scale between boutique and generalist emerged:

Big training companies	very generalist on the whole – claim to be experts in most fields
Business schools	very generalist on the whole – claim to be experts in most fields
Government/business support agencies	very generalist on the whole – claim to be experts in most fields
Independents	Very specialist, usually
MCP	Very specialist

Axis 2: style

A scale between theoretical/research/agenda-based training and highly practical/challenging emerged:

Big training companies	driven by the teaching agenda
Business schools	driven by the teaching agenda
Government/business support agencies	usually driven by the teaching agenda
Independents	driven by the teaching agenda as well as listening to client needs
MCP	obsessed by the clients' needs

If you plot the two axes onto a matrix and plot the various positions of the differing competitors your map should look like this.

Brand Positioning Matrix

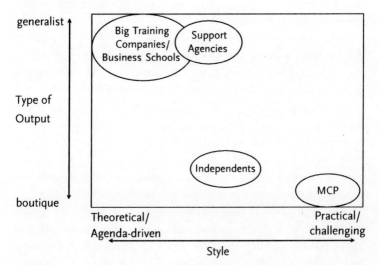

What you can see from the positioning matrix is that your selection of axes has enabled us to define a unique positioning. This can be used to emphasise the difference between the business and its competitors.

For instance, your advertising copy or sales pitch could run along the lines of, 'Whereas most training companies are focused on their own teaching agenda, we are quite the opposite. We focus on client needs.' Or, 'If you want a generalist training company, go to the others. But, if you want a training company that is more interested in a deep understanding of the subject of leadership, then come to us!'

The positioning task enables you to define your own niche. And the purpose of developing your niche is to make your business different, or even unique, in its category.

At its simplest level, you decide the titles of the axes. The purpose is to find axes that emphasise the difference between you and your competitors (in the eyes of the customer).

What to put on the axes? It is time for a bit of creativity here. Look at your business through your customers' eyes. If you interviewed a customer, what might be the criteria that they would use to measure you, as compared with others in your industry? For example, would you be smarter, faster, higher-tech, more rigorous, cheaper, cleaner, friendlier?

Take several of the criteria that might be applied to your business and see which ones create some kind of a space between you and the competition. For instance, if the criterion is 'fast', does this suggest that most of your competitors are much slower? If the criterion is 'younger', does this suggest that your competition is mostly much older?

Eventually you will have two criteria for the two axes. You might have: bespoke–standard solution; local–national; traditional–hyper-modern, hi-tech–lo-tech; metropolitan–provincial; indoors–outdoors; cheap–expensive; people-led–market-led; and so on.

You need to go through the motions of doing this on paper. Reading about it will not make you get a better understanding of your business. Finding the right combination of axes is the tough part. If you are able to separate yourself from 'the rest', then this becomes the difference that you can focus on.

A brand-positioning statement

Having attempted the positioning exercise, you can use the results to create or develop your brand-positioning statement, a simple one-page summary of the key elements that make up your brand personality and your brand proposition. This 'worksheet' helps your thinking about what attributes your brand should be carrying.

The thinking about the issues is probably more important than the final output. The process considers establishing what you are and what you are not. It helps to define what you want your brand to represent.

Your brand-positioning statement should consider the following. Looking at the case study below, you can then fill in your own Brand-Positioning Statement.

- **Market description**: Describes the marketplace that the brand is meant to be living in. It is the market description that customers would use: for example, retail sports goods, construction materials.

- **Target audience**: Pinpoints the people whom you are trying to get to look at your brand, the people you are selling to: for example, sports players, builders' merchants.

- **Brand discriminators**: Describes what benefits the brand is best at delivering: for example, honest advice, reliable delivery.

- **Core customer proposition**: Refers to the emotional and functional aspects of what is being offered to the customer: for example, security, confidence.

- **Brand differentiators**: Considers how the brand is different: for example, all staff qualified, unique guarantees.

- **Brand personality**: Is about the image and associations that it should create: for example, fit and sporty, reliable and trustworthy.

Case study: The BPS

Below is the BPS as created for the Directors' Centre.

Brand-positioning statement

Market description:	consultancy
Target audience:	blue-chip businesses; senior managers
Brand discriminators:	honest, practical
Core customer proposition: theory	practical, straightforward, not high
Brand differentiator:	focus on entrepreneurship
Brand personality:	challenging, open, ethical

Brand-positioning statement (BPS)

Market description:

Target audience:

Brand discriminators:

Core customer proposition:

Brand differentiator:

Brand personality:

Summary

Probably the most powerful tool in the marketing arsenal is actually the ability to be absolutely clear about what it is that you are offering – *you* can decide how the buying public will see you. As the customer is king (in the long run), you must put yourself in a position where the customer wishes to buy from you and not one of your competitors.

Positioning enables you to decide, design and deliver how you wish to be seen. If it is good enough for Madonna then I am sure that it is good enough for you!

23: The Seven-Point *Customer is King* Plan – 6: Calculate Just How Much a Customer is Worth to You

Do you know how much a customer is worth to you?

- An introduction to relationship marketing (RM).
- The concept of the lifetime value of the customer.

Question

Unless you know the true value of a customer (to your business), how can you decide how much you are prepared to spend to acquire one?

Relationship marketing

Customers are often worth more to us than we realise. This is particularly true in the case of services. What follows is an introduction to relationship marketing and the key concept of customer lifetime value.

Definition

'Relationship marketing' is about maximising long-term profitability through the intelligent use of information. The information is used to enhance and to create superior relationships with customers.

Is it something for the smaller and growing business?

Relationship marketing, to my mind, involves customising and developing the offer that you make. As a result, you also develop your dialogue with the client to maximise the value to them. It is more sophisticated than the traditional marketing process: it makes customers feel valued because it responds to their individual circumstances. In effect, it is marketing with a memory.

The key phrases associated with relationship marketing are:

> - Customer lifetime value – looking at income, cost and profit over the full period of the relationship rather than just on an annual basis.
>
> - Data warehousing – the collection into one place of information from many places.
>
> - Data mining – the process of searching for nuggets of valuable information that can provide ideas for enhancing value or for extraordinarily persuasive communications.

Relationship marketing is mainly propagated in larger businesses (where the budgets to pay the consultants exist!). However, on a small scale, this way of behaviour is the instinctive approach of all smaller businesses, especially when they are young. After all, relationships and service are often the strong competitive advantage of the smaller or growing businesses. Just look at smaller businesses that are in some kind of niche.

In some senses, with smaller volumes of clients, it is easier for the smaller business to think through ways to develop the relationship with the client. After all, no real marketing expertise is required. But do remember that relationship marketing is not a remedial strategy: it assumes that you are already doing well; it is strategy for growth and not for turnaround.

And when is it applicable?

Relationship marketing is particularly good when there is a single decision maker or when there is a large volume of customers with varying needs. It also works well when customers are not actively account-managed by a salesperson, and when the high costs of customer acquisition (getting customers) makes loyalty a key goal or where the exchange of information between the buyer and seller is crucial or where it is possible to differentiate your product through the quality of your service.

Testing suitability for customer relationship marketing

Jim McLaughlin, my friend and colleague at The Directors' Centre, uses this ten-point questionnaire to assess suitability.

1. What are the drivers in the market? Can you deliver increased competitive advantage by creating higher levels of loyalty?
2. How many customers does the business have? Is it clear what a customer is?
3. What is the retention level? If extremely good, it makes relationship marketing less compelling.
4. Do customers buy from more than one supplier? Do they have to? How good is our 'share of the customer'? How will CRM improve it?
5. Do we have the IT/marketing/accounting skills to run a more than competent CRM programme?
6. Do we have the money to invest in the programme?
7. Do we have the right data? Where can we get it from?
8. Are we already doing a good job for the customer? Can we also improve on this?
9. Does the company have a customer ethos that will maintain and sustain any improvements?
10. Are our existing campaigns well executed?

Customer lifetime value

Customer lifetime value is at the heart of relationship marketing. Data warehousing and data mining are the tools used in bigger businesses.

In traditional marketing, each client is valued on a year-by-year basis, focusing on profit per annum. This approach creates a gap between the measurement system and the real world. In the real world it may take some time to make a customer profitable. Remember, customers do not stop and start with the financial year. It may take several years for your investment in a relationship to pay off.

Customer lifetime value is a way of considering the customer across their anticipated life as a customer of the company. It acknowledges that the investment a company makes in acquiring a new customer would probably not be repaid with the first purchase or – even the first year of purchases!

Case study: The cost of acquiring a client

Jay Bradbury Photographic Studios specialises in fulfilling all photographic needs for local businesses and organisation. Jay estimates that each new account will stay with him, for, on average, three years. Each account will give him one assignment per month at an average fee of £500. So the lifetime income from a new client can be expected to be £18,000.

With a gross margin of 30 per cent, one new account will generate £5,400. Hence Jay has calculated that even if he spent £3,600 trying to acquire a client then it would still be money well spent because this would still give him an average net margin of 10 per cent (£1,800).

LIFETIME VALUE OF A CUSTOMER CALCULATOR

On average, a new customer will buy from the business for _____ years.

And, on average, a new customer will generate _____ orders per year.

The average value of an order is £_____.

So, Lifetime Income from a new customer is:

___years × ___orders pa × £___ order value = £_____.

Therefore, with an average Gross Margin of ___%,

A new customer will generate a Lifetime Gross Margin of:

Summary

Until you know what a potential client might be worth to you, you cannot accurately decide how much you should spend trying to acquire them.

There are plenty of books that go into great detail about the best weapons that you should use to drive your marketing campaign. Here is a brief list of some of the key tools that you may find appropriate for enhancing the customer experience.

■ You can think about how to spend your marketing budget only after you know whom you are trying to reach and what you are trying to say to them.

My view is simple.

Opinion

Unless you know what you are trying to communicate and to whom and why, then you cannot effectively choose the most appropriate tools. Don't think about which tools (or weapons) you might use until you have figured out exactly what you are trying to communicate to whom and against whom.

My intention in this book is to help you to understand what your customers want so that you can give it to them. As part of this process you will need to choose the appropriate communication tools. What follows is a brief list of available tools. This list has been well documented elsewhere and is not the main focus of this book.

■ **Advertising**: Small ads, Yellow Pages, radio/TV ads, mid-air, banners, co-operative.

- **Paper media**: Cards, low-cost brochures, video, banners, bumper stickers, circulars, posters, newsletters, gift certificates, reward cards, your order forms, positioning with stationery.
- **Internet**: Website, banner advertising, affiliate programmes, discussion forums, co-operatives, e-business.
- **Targeted media**: Mailing lists, postcards, inserts, direct mail, catalogues.
- **Promotion**: Contests, sweepstakes, frequent buyer plans, jingles, slogans, packaging POS (point of sale), special gifts, trade shows, free publicity.
- **Telephone**: Telephone music, 0800 numbers, toll-free, advertising messages.
- **Nonmedia**: Price setting, business name, agents, minorities, word of mouth, viral, testimonials, accessibility, speed, service, using customer research, conference speaking.

Summary

You cannot start to choose your marketing weapons until you have clarity about who you are trying to attract and with which method. Most marketing campaigns start with a budget, then select tools and then choose the message. This is a totally upside-down way of looking at the problem (unless you enjoy spending other people's money).

PART THREE |

25: The Immutable Laws of Customer-Focused Marketing (for new and growing businesses)

In the following chapter I have stated what I consider to be the immutable laws of marketing. They apply specifically to new and growing businesses that need plain, common sense and no-nonsense marketing help. They appear in no particular order.

> ■ Sixteen laws that help you to understand why you are (or are not) successful in your efforts to attract and retain customers.

Never forget what it feels like to be a customer. When being sold to, customers have a little voice in their heads, a mantra, which repeats the same things again and again:

> ■ 'Don't waste our time.'
> ■ 'Remember who we are.'
> ■ 'Make it easy for us to order and procure service.'
> ■ 'Make sure your service delights us!'
> ■ 'Customise your products and service for me!'

Attitude check

In the words of Rick Dobbins in *The Ultimate Entrepreneur's Book*, if you believe, and many do, that customers are essentially . . .

- lazy
- ignorant
- selfish
- greedy
- vain
- disloyal

... then you have been reading the wrong book! And, even if these *are* your beliefs, then to be successful you will still need to be:

- opportunistic
- energetic
- helpful
- generous
- self-effacing

To make the customer feel like a king or queen, you will need the high-level and low-level involvement of every employee in achieving excellent customer value, very efficiently, for high profit.

And, on that basis, I have put together the Immutable Laws of Customer-Focused Marketing with the assistance of my friend and colleague, Timothy Cumming.

The sixteen Immutable Laws

1: The Law of Perception
Marketing is a battle of perceptions and not simply a battle of products.
Most people seem to assume that, in the battle for customers, it is the best product that wins. This is clearly not the case. The winner is the product that customers *believe* to be the best as proven by whether or not they buy.

While the product's quality or features may play an important part in the buying decision, there are many forms of persuasion that will have influenced their thinking – brand image, company reputation or competitor comparisons, to name but a few, and all of these are perceived. The job in hand is to win over the customer's mind.

2: The Law of Questions
Questions lead to answers; answers lead to relationships; relationships lead to profit.

One of the easiest ways to put the customer first is to ask questions continually (and to respect the customer's answers). The more you ask, the more competitive advantage you gain, and the stronger your customer relationships become. And nothing succeeds in cementing customer relations like advice heeded – just watch their reaction to a new product feature that they suggested! To make the customer feel in control, ask the right questions to find what they want from you.

3: The Law of Precision
The ability to define accurately your precise market segments dramatically affects your profitability. So segment carefully!

Divide your markets into slices that are distinctive, profitable and suit your strengths. Ditch the rest and really concentrate on just those segments. It'll save you money on promotion and production/operations and will strengthen your sales messages. Figure out whom you can really delight.

4: The Law of Different Missions for Different Positions
Your strategies depend upon your position.

If you fail to be Number One in the prospect's mind then you have to adopt different strategies. In Number Two position, you must differentiate yourself from the Number One, otherwise you just look like a pale imitation.

The best way to separate yourself is to focus on the differences, the opposites. For instance, you might say, 'We are professional and thorough, so sometimes things will take a little longer – it's worth the wait', 'If you don't want to be treated like a number . . .', 'We offer fixed-price packages' and so on.

Use the appropriate strategy for your position.

5: The Law of Time
Marketing returns exist in the long term.

Be aware that short-term gains (sales today) may be at the cost of the longer-term game. Your 'offer' must be consistent and it must be consistently consistent. A sale price may imply that you are overcharging at other times – the result is reduced future sales at the premium rates as punters wait for the next sale offer.

Be aware of the relationship between the long term and the short term. Short-term gains seem fine, but at what cost? Decide your goals and be prepared to pay the price (probably in advance). If you want to put the customer in control, be honest about the trade-offs.

6: The Integration Law
Marketing is nothing if it is not company wide.

If the marketing or sales people are the only ones carrying the marketing flag, you're in trouble! Customers will read your marketing messages as loose promises and hot air if the reality isn't as glittering as the claims. Plan and relate the marketing aspects of every business activity for the whole company.

Educate your production or operations people, your office manager and your receptionist so that they understand their role in putting the customer first. At the very least, that means convenience, speed, hospitality, choice, proactivity, manners and honesty.

7: The Law of the Driving Seat
The management team is the centre for improvement.

You won't pull off miraculous improvements from anywhere else. Drive all your marketing programmes from the management team. Get everybody involved – but make it your priority to drive the programme from the top. Otherwise other priorities will take over, practical hurdles will get in the way and your marketing development will sink in a swamp of mediocrity.

8: The Law of Measurement

Don't just measure: interpret.

Sure, measure all you can – an objective isn't worth the paper it's written on if you can't track your progress towards it. But don't be a bean-counter. Analyse the results – interpret them for meaningful trends or comparisons: '48 per cent increase in demand for after-sales care' may be interpreted as 'the product needs tweaking, and clients want stronger relationships'.

9 : The First Law

If you aren't Number One in your existing category, then create your own category, or be the first in their minds.

People love to buy from Number One in the category; they believe that Number One is better than the rest (otherwise why would they be Number One?). So you can always be 'Best in the West', 'the First Mexican Takeaway', the 'Original One-Stop Shop', 'the Only Printers With a Money-Back Guarantee' and so forth. If customers love the leader, then find a way to lead.

But all is not lost if you can't be first in the category. With a simpler name to remember or a new product (better, quicker, cheaper, faster or nicer), suddenly you've taken poll position in their minds. It is amazing how the mind allows only two or three key names to be associated with a product or service. That's why new names can knock one of the older and less 'active' big names off the top of the list, suddenly becoming a household name (Dyson cleaners are a prime example). If the new kid on the block can make a lasting impression, then they may be able to steal a march on the so-called 'old and trusted'. Big names be warned – we live in a changing world and you cannot afford to rest on your laurels, especially if you've been at the top of the league for some time.

10: The Law of Tricky Extensions

The irresistible urge to extend product lines or move into new markets may be self-defeating in the long run – 'brand equity', when stretched, usually gets spread more thinly.

A good brand and reputation for one product or service doesn't necessarily extend to a new range or market. Some brands can do it

– and at what price? – and others cannot. Be aware of just how difficult it is to do something you are not really expert in and don't kid yourself otherwise.

A café by day thinks it can do outside catering or posh evening meals; a delicatessen thinks it can run a sandwich round. When you go into a new market or product area you just 'don't know what you don't know' – always assess the opportunity rationally.

11: Pareto's Law
The 80:20 Rule is everywhere – to be effective, cut back on the ineffective and focus on the effective efforts.
Pareto's 80:20 Principle is everywhere we look: 80 per cent of profits come from 20 per cent of customers; 80 per cent of sales come from 20 per cent of the sales force; and, conversely, 20 per cent of profits would come from 80 per cent of customers. If you want to work smarter, focus on the highly effective and ignore the rest.

Draw a line below your Top 20 per cent of clients and inform the rest of new prices to give you margins similar to those with the profitable clients. Some will 'play the game', which is fine, and some will not, which is fine also, because you don't want their business in the first place. Who wants to be a busy fool?

So find out the characteristics of your Top 20 per cent and find some more customers like them.

12: The Laws of Success and Failure
Success and failure go hand in hand – it's OK to make mistakes but you must learn from your mistakes. And remember: nothing succeeds like success.
Failure is part of learning: if you didn't fail occasionally then you wouldn't be taking enough risks. Recognise a failure and cut your losses before disaster ensues. It is only the 'English way' that is so unforgiving of business failure. How else do you find out if an idea can work if you don't experiment? The question is the price that you might have to pay.

Success can be as damaging as failure. Healthy bank balances and being Number One in league tables make organisations arrogant, big-headed and sluggish; they start to believe in myths, and, when the emperor's new clothes are seen for what they are by the customers, the competition move in and steal the action.

You are at your most vulnerable when you are Number One: everyone wants to knock you off your perch and will be able to undercut your prices to win some work away from you. Customers start to use you as a reference point but may be able to buy a similar-looking product at a lower price.

13: The Law of Reversibility
Start with the end in mind, and accept responsibility for the results.
If you start with your end in mind, then you are able to picture the stepping stones to getting there, because, looking back from the visualised scenario, you can see what will need to be done. This is a far more productive way of planning the future as it points out all the potential hurdles along the way. It also focuses the mind on cause and effect. Remember, there are reasons why customers will buy or refuse your products and services. Understand that you can determine the effects that you want but that this requires dedication and planning.

14: The 'P-FAB-P' Law
Customers buy benefits and proofs – show them the advantages and features but make sure the benefits and proofs address their problem.
See things through the customers' eyes. As the saying goes, if you want to understand a Red Indian, spend a day walking in his/her moccasins. When looking through the customers' eyes always think, What's in it for me? 'P-FAB-P' refers to Problem, Features, Advantages, Benefits and Proofs. As producers we get preoccupied with what we put into the product (the features). Customers are much more interested in what is in it for them (they focus on benefits) and how we can demonstrate these benefits (the proofs). Every sales pitch should employ the words 'Which means that . . .'

to ensure that you are explaining how your product will solve your customer's problem.

15: The Law of PLC
The Product Life Cycle will haunt you in all your work.

Just about every product in the long run will go through a series of stages of growth (conception, birth, growing pains, development, adolescence, maturity and death). You can try to extend or reinvigorate any particular phase but the law will not go away. Understanding that the law does exist enables you to design your strategy to reflect or resist the current stage that you are in.

Remember also the difference between a fad and a trend – fads tend to be short-lived (although the Law of PLC suggests that a fad can return, albeit in a reincarnated state, in a cyclical fashion).

16: The Law of KISS
KISS = Keep It Simple, Stupid.

Marketing can be hugely effective as long as you don't make it too clever or sophisticated – complexity does not help the customer.

Summary

The Sixteen Immutable Laws of Customer-Focused Marketing

1: The Law of Perception
2: The Law of Questions
3: The Law of Precision
4: The Law of Different Missions For Different Positions
5: The Law of Time
6: The Integration Law
7: The Law of the Driving Seat
8: The Law of Measurement
9: The First Law
10: The Law of Tricky Extensions
11: Pareto's Law

26: Crunch Questions on Customer-Focused Marketing

Good questions can elicit good, thoughtful and insightful answers. Bad questions tend to generate bad answers.

- Crunch questions.
- Some excellent one-liners to give you some food for thought.

The goal is to be able to select the right questions at the right time. Here is a list of questions that I find incredibly powerful – they precipitate a further analysis of a series of issues and often challenge a series of assumptions, a shaky foundation, upon which a whole empire may have been built.

These questions can be used by the business owner or by an adviser. Several questions can be selected and act as the starting point for an exploratory discussion about the business. Alternatively, you may like to ponder the real answers to these questions. Do not simply give the glib, off-the-cuff answers, but think carefully about what your answers actually imply for the business.

1. What business are you really in?

2. Where do you make the money?

3. How good are your competitive positions?

4. Is this a good industry to be in?

5. What do your customers think?

6. How do you raise profits quickly?

7. How do you build long-term value?

8. What do you do differently from other businesses?

9. What investments underpin your differences?

10. What are your key sources of competitive advantage?

11. What do you need to do to make a difference?

12. What must you keep? What must you lose?

13. How could you simplify your business so that you could raise value by at least 50 per cent?

14. Isn't your strategy rather complex? Aren't all great strategies very simple?

15. What is the key idea, your business concept?

16. Who is your target customer, your client base?

17. What do you really know about them?

18. Can you describe a typical customer in detail?

19. What problem are you solving?

20. Why do people buy your product at all?

21. Why do people buy your product from you?

22. Why does your typical customer buy from you?

23. Which clients are cool?

24. Which clients drive you mad?

25. Should you be working with them?

26. What benefits are you offering that your competition doesn't?

27. If you could use just two sentences to describe what your business stands for, what would they be?

28. What is your company known for?

29. What's your value proposition to customers that they can't get anywhere else?

30. Who are your most profitable customers?

31. At what rate do they leave you?

32. Why do they leave?

33. What is the call to action? What do you want your (potential) customers to do?

34. Who is your most serious competitor?

35. What are their plans?

36. And what are their costs, profits?

37. Do you really know what customers think about you?

38. Who are currently just new/minor threats?

39. Do you have a product/service that is sharply different from that of your competitors?

40. Are you supplying the right things? And in the most effective way? And at the lowest possible economic cost?

41. Are you as good as or better than your best competitor?

42. Are you serving the widest possible market?

43. Are you in some way unique? Is there a reason why people should buy from you rather than from someone else?

44. Would God have a good laugh if he saw your marketing plan?

45. What keeps you awake at night about your business?

46. What are your objectives? What are you trying to achieve?

47. What will enable you to overcome the barriers, and/or achieve the objectives?

48. If you had a magic wand, what changes would you make to the business?

49. What is stopping you from making your magic wand changes now?

50. What three things are the most critical to the success of the business?

51. Which 20 per cent of product/service makes 80 per cent of profit?

52. Who are your top five customers and how much contribution did they generate last month?

53. Which customers are unprofitable?

54. On which products should you raise the selling price now?

55. Which underperforming product lines should you drop now?

56. Which product lines should you concentrate on selling more?

57. What is success for you?

58. What is success for the business?

59. What does your business stand for?

60. Is what you are doing exciting? Or challenging? Or just plain dull, average and mediocre?

61. So what is it that you do that is so exciting?

62. Does what you do, matter?

63. How could you raise the impact?

64. Are you pushing or leading or goading your clients?

65. If your business were an animal, what would it be and why?

66. What animal would you *wish* your business to be and why?

67. What do you need to do to get your business from being the animal that it is to being the animal that you wish it were?

68. If your business were an island, what sort of island would it be?

69. Running your business is like riding a bicycle because . . .?

70. If you could work half-time, what would you do to double your profit?

71. What would Richard Branson do if he took over your business?

72. What would your closest rival do if they took over your business?

73. How can you get luckier?

74. What excuses do you tend to use?

And some crunch one-liners to give you some food for thought

Brand it

You cannot *not* communicate your brand. Everything about your business communicates something. So what is it that you want to be communicating? First, decide what it is that you wish to communicate and to whom. Remember whom you are doing this for.

Brand *you*

Treat yourself as a business treats its brand. You need to plan and create a strategy for communicating what it is that you represent, what it is that you do, where you want to be seen and what you want to be known for. What is your Unique Selling Point (USP)? To focus on the customer, focus on your personal relationship with them.

Sort it. Stop procrastinating – do it now

Stop procrastinating. Sometimes it is better to make a decision, one way or the other and look at the results, rather than make no decision at all. Paralysis by analysis is the disease of the undecided and the uncommitted.

Keep it

Don't make changes for change's sake. If it ain't broke, don't fix it. We spend too much time re-creating and re-engineering things that are perfectly OK.

Get your customers' permission to sell to them

Traditional mass-selling techniques are simply not effective and have low success rates. Look for customers to give you permission to stay in contact with them. Customers who have given you permission to have a relationship with them are ten times more likely to spend money with you.

People love to buy from people, but they hate to be sold at

In today's one-to-one marketing world, customers hate to be *sold at* by badly trained salespeople. But customers love to *buy* products *from* you. Seduce them to your business (and treat them like royalty), but do not treat them like morons.

Work the 80:20 principle

The principle of the vital few and the trivial many: 80 per cent of profits come from 20 per cent of customers; 20 per cent of profits come from 80 per cent of customers. If you want to work smarter, focus on the highly effective and ignore the rest!

Strategy is all about trade-offs

Strategy is all about planning while being aware of the business environment. Strategy is about being clear about what you do and what you don't do.

Create marketing space

Separate yourself from the competition. Make yourself different.

Remove your self-limiting beliefs

What limits have you set for yourself subconsciously? You are what you believe. If you believe that you cannot swim, then you will not be able to swim. If you believe that you are frightened of flying then you will be frightened of flying. How do you limit yourself?

Stop unprofitable activity

Do you know how profitable you are, by customer, by product, by channel? And if it ain't profitable then why are you doing it? What excuses are you using to continue to do unprofitable work?

Focus on the important

Know the difference between what is urgent and what is important. You must know which things are really important to you or to your business. And, if you know what is really important, then you know what is less important and what is really unimportant. What excuses do you use to work on anything but the most important?

Be first in the customer's mind – and if you can't be first in a category then create a new category

People love to buy from Number One.

Feel the fear and do it anyway

Fear is a perfectly natural emotion. If you aren't sailing close to the wind then you are probably not taking enough risks. Acknowledge the fear and make a calculated decision. Use the adrenaline and energy that the fear creates to work for you rather than against you.

Infect your staff

Infect your staff with an enthusiasm and excitement for your customers and for the business. Make your staff involved; do not treat them like fools but with the respect that they deserve. After all, you can't live out any of your dreams on your own – you need your people to do it for you.

Infect your customers

Delight your customers. Your customers are your most powerful marketing tool. They can get you more business than any multi-million-pound advertising campaign. Get your customers talking about you and being proud to be associated with you and your company.

Seek first to understand, and then to be understood

You have two ears and two eyes but one mouth. When communicating use them in that ratio. Listen, look and speak. You need to understand where your audience are coming from before you can help them. To do any less is highly presumptuous.

Work *on*, not *in*, your business
When Ray Kroc started McDonald's, he never intended to work *in* the business cooking hamburgers: he always intended to work on *growing* the business. If you work *in* the business then you cannot work *on* the business. How much time do you need to spend working on the business rather than in the business?

Spend more time thinking and less time doing
As you rise up through an organisation you will progressively spend more and more of your time thinking and less and less of your time doing. The role of the leader of an organisation is to spend time looking down on what is going on and taking the broad view.

Less is more – simplify everything
The simpler the concept, the more power it has. Use your time and your resources with care.

Cut the excuses – just do it
You can always find a reason for not doing something, or putting off till tomorrow what you should do today. There's no excuse: get on with it.

Actions speak louder than words
You cannot get 'there' by planning alone – you have to take action.

We are what we repeatedly do
They are the words of Aristotle, who added, 'Success, then, is not an act, but a habit.'

You rarely increase quality by reducing costs
You often reduce costs by increasing quality.

Ask stupid questions
Think the unthinkable and say the unsayable – how else will you be different from your competition?

It always costs more to put things right than to get things right

Stop helping people – let them fail

Only by making their own mistakes will your people learn.

Don't shy away from passion

If you believe in what you're doing, you needn't feel shy about becoming passionate about it.

27: Delivering the Promise

- Self-imposed doubt and management-affirmed doubt will undermine your finest efforts.
- Be aware of fundamental gaps in communication and perception in your business.
- To succeed you need to 'go for it'. It's no easy task.

Delivering your promise is all about people, organisation and systems. Chris Daffy, in *Once a Customer, Always a Customer*, talks about 'SID' and 'MADness' – these two acronyms are what will get in the way of your business success. Ignore them at your peril.

SID

SID stands for Self-Imposed Doubt.

Like a disease, SID can spread through an organisation. Listen to the victim language that experienced SIDs like to use:

- 'I can't make a difference.'
- 'It would never work like that around here.'
- 'I was involved in an initiative like this once before and that didn't work.'
- 'All this is going to mean more work for me.'
- 'No one will notice; no one really cares.'

It's a bit like having a poison-tongued monkey that sits on our shoulder: we can get indoctrinated to believe that all change is bad. You know what a mantra is – well this is a 'can't-ra':

> ■ 'I can't do this.'
> ■ 'I can't do better.'

To turn the message from can't to can – from a 'can't-ra' to a 'can-tra' – weed out the people who are trying to infect the others.

MADness

All of us have experienced MADness – Management Affirmed Doubt. You hear managers in companies infected with MADness saying things like:

> ■ 'You can't make a difference.'
> ■ 'Your ideas would never work like that around here.'
> ■ 'We were involved in an initiative like this once before and that didn't work.'
> ■ 'All this is going to mean more work for you.'
> ■ 'We doubt if we'll notice; we don't really care in any case.'

Managers who practise this madness must be sorted out fast.

While in the land of three-letter acronyms, I will refer to one more. Andy Gilbert uses the phrase 'Go MAD' in his book of the same name. For Andy, 'MAD' means 'Make A Difference'. At the heart of change is our capacity to make a difference – a difference to the lives of our colleagues, our customers and our family and friends. So, a clarion call is just that – Go MAD, Go Make A Difference.

Mind the gap

As you step off the underground train the announcer calls, 'Mind the gap!' You must mind the gaps in your business:

> ■ the gap between what you think the customer wants and what the customer really wants
> ■ the gap between what you think you offer and what the customer thinks/believes that you offer

- the gap between the expectations that you create for the customer and the actual service that you deliver
- the gap between what you promise and what you deliver
- the gap between what management think is going on and what is really going on

Learning point

You must establish the difference between your perception and that of the customer. Otherwise you are on a road to nowhere!

Marketing courage: enthusiasm, energy and passion

Books on marketing make a great read. They are all about the rosy future when customers are attracted to your business like bees to a honey pot. The reality is usually somewhat different. To get your marketing right is tough. It requires serious thought and a commitment of your two most valuable assets: your time and your money.

It is a brave person who follows through his or her marketing plans. What starts off as an idea or a whim is researched and developed until a final marketing plan is produced. As the plan is analysed, assessed and tested, we tend to water down our ambitious first intentions. The real trick is to have the guts to follow through on your instincts. By all means check them, but at the end of the day halfway is *no* way! In my opinion, you should be brave and 'go for it'!

The marketing courage that I refer to is rarely seen in large organisations – the daring ideas that advertising agencies present inevitably get diluted as they pass through committees and as employees consider how their actions might be perceived by their superiors. It is in the smaller business, where your future may depend on the success of your marketing, that you see real marketing courage. The guts boldly to attack a market sector and risk the potential failure is a true act of bravery.

In essence, what supports and nurtures this bravery is a sense of purpose. This sense of purpose is an energy that may even border on obsession. The energy and passion for your product can separate you from your competition. If personal relationships are crucial in the relationship-development and sales cycle then clearly the conviction and belief of the sales team becomes crucial. Energy and passion behind a well-positioned and effective product are a powerful combination. If memorable sensory experiences are a crucial part of the rewarding purchase then your commitment and attention to your relationship with the potential customer will add to the feelings they have from dealing with you!

You need courage to:

- Tell people what you are going to do.
- Set stretching, challenging goals that you don't know how to achieve (yet)!
- Tell people that you will deliver.
- Stand out from the rest.
- Be proud of your work.
- Be convinced that your business is better than the rest.
- Lead your people with enthusiasm, passion and conviction.
- Belive that the way everyone else does things isn't always the right way (six million flies aren't necessarily right about one piece of cow dung!).
- Believe that you are doing the right thing.

Getting started

Here are some thoughts to get you from thinking about doing stuff for the customer to actually doing it:

- Find the biggest 'pain point' and then go to work to fix it.
- Measure the right stuff! The balanced business scorecard (see Glossary) is perfect for this kind of thing. It makes you look at efficiency, effectiveness and customer satisfaction. With the scorecard you are able to draw the link between customer satisfaction and profitability.

- Bring people inside the organisation together, around the question, 'How do we want this company to deal with customers?' Create principles for how you are going to run the business. A simple idea but people rarely do it.

- Make the customer experience effortless and fun!

- Focus on key customers by role. Use a tool called 'customer scenario mapping': pick three to six scenarios for each area in which customers are having problems doing business with you; next map out how customers would rather do things. This process tells you what matters most to people and where you should put your effort. Tactical, simple and can start on Monday.

- Use risk reversal as a tool to limit customer risk: you guarantee 100 per cent satisfaction or offer their money back – it's a great and very seductive offer.

- Use complaints as the big entrance to wooing and delighting customers.

- Let your customers shop the way they want to shop!

The biggest secret to business success is always to maintain an edge in everything that you do. One of the biggest competitive edges you will have is if you make it easier for the client to say 'yes' than to say 'no'. If you take away the financial, psychological, physical and emotional risk factors then you get a powerful advantage over the competition. You make the customer feel great (they can't lose, you carry the risk, and if they are delighted they'll keep coming back to you for more).

ACTION POINT: Removing obstacles

Make a list of every obstacle that you and your staff create to stop and discourage people from buying from you.

Divide the list into financial, emotional and measurability reasons. Ask why you shouldn't offer your services where you carry all the risk (such as with a money-back guarantee).

If you do provide a high-quality and high-value service that can be appreciated and recognised, then don't be afraid to offer a risk reversal. The option will encourage more customers to 'take a chance' with you – they will feel that they are in control because they can walk away from the relationship when they feel like it. They feel better, and probably buy more.

Summary

Go for it!

28: The Frequently Asked Questions

1. How can I get more customers?
It may not be more customers that you want. It may be that you really need more profitable (i.e. better) customers. To get more customers you need to know:

- who they are
- what they want
- where to find them
- whom you are competing against

Think about what it is that you are actually trying to achieve – volume, profits, market share? More customers may not be the answer, as you may simply become a 'busy fool'. The answer is rarely found in lowering your prices, as this destroys your profit margins.

2. How can I get better customers?
In reply, I ask, 'What do you mean by "better customers"?' It may be that you want more loyal customers who are happy to pay premium prices for your product; this is not unusual. Some research is required to understand how you can add value to the customer's experience and how you can find people willing to pay the premium.

3. How much should I spend on my website?
My question to you is, 'Should you have a website at all?' What do you want your website to do? How long will it take for you to get a

return on your investment? While I do not wish to knock the work of web-design companies, I have had several websites designed for me for less than $1,000 each. I went to the local art college degree show; I looked at the students' work and invited one to design and build my website – it has been recommended for awards and cost me twenty times less than similar websites (have a look at www.robert-craven.com).

So you can make websites for a low cost – the key is to have an absolutely clear brief in terms of what you are trying to say and to whom. (Have a look at Timothy Cumming's *Little e, Big Commerce*, also in this series.)

4. How can I improve my advertising effectiveness?
Test and measure everything that you do. Try looking at some of Jay Abraham's books on guerrilla marketing – think about what you are trying to achieve and see if there isn't a cheaper or more effective or more innovative way of doing it. Have a look at Jurgen Wolff's *Do Something Different*, in this series.

5. How can I stop being a busy fool?
Sit down and work out the difference between what is important and what is just urgent. Step back and take a helicopter view. Decide what you want and focus on it. Learn to say 'no'. Take responsibility for your own actions!

6. How can I decide my prices?
Ask your customers. Compare yourself with your competitors. Be clear about the margins that you need to achieve. Know your break-even point. Be clear about how your business's finances interrelate (costs–profits–volume). Have a look at my friend, Paul Barrow's *The Bottom Line* (also published in this series).

7. How should I decide whether to put up prices?
To quote H George Selfridge (the retailer), 'Get the confidence of the public and you will have no difficulty getting their patronage ... Remember always that the recollection of quality remains long after the price is forgotten.'

8. How do I know if my marketing is working?

Set targets, test, monitor and measure all activities. Don't take anything for granted. Get the whole business to obsess about the customer. Create objectives and performance measures; don't assume that you'll ever get it right. Keep looking for smarter, better ways to seduce customers and to keep them with you.

9. How can I get to know what it's like to be a customer?

Ask them what it feels like. Carry out market-research surveys, customer surveys, take them out for dinner. Most important of all, just listen to them. They normally tell you what you are doing wrong and what you are doing right. After all, you can't expect to be a mind reader. And reward them for the help that they give you. Make the customers feel like part of the team.

10. Customers, clients, consumers – what's the difference, and who cares?

When talking about the sales process it helps to understand the difference between these similar concepts. Customers buy products for cash or over the counter and pay before use. Clients tend to get invoiced after use of a product/service. Consumers are the people who actually receive the product or service and they may not be the same as the people who pay for it.

There is an argument that anyone who buys from you should be thought of as a client because this implies developing a long-term relationship and not just a single transaction that is implied by the use of the word 'customer'.

11. How can I make my staff really care about the customer?

Lead by example. Reward brilliant customer service. Don't employ people who don't understand the concept. Train them. Put the customer first at all times. Recognise the long-term benefits of a customer fixation.

12. Won't trying to make my customer king be a never-ending and expensive exercise?

Maybe. If you are not moving faster than your competition then you should not be surprised if your customers desert you. Change is everywhere and it is the norm – do not expect things to stay still, unless you work in a waxworks. Customer-obsessive behaviour is not expensive when you consider how expensive it is to run an unfocused mediocre, run-of-the-mill business.

13. Are customers always right?

No they are not, but very often they are. We all get the occasional poisoned dwarf who will never be happy with your product or service. The sooner they move on to your competitors, the better. Beg them to leave you, pay them if need be but get rid of them because these customers take up a disproportionate amount of your time, efforts and emotions. You do not want these people associated with your business at any price.

14. Where is the magic formula in this book?

You won't find it on any one page. The magic formula for your business is in your head. This book can only present a series of ideas, thoughts and challenges to you. The precise formula, strategy and method of delivery that are right for your customers are what you have got to figure out. That is why this book has not taken a full-on prescriptive approach. Good Luck!

Postscript

An early draft of this book included a 'Hall of Shame', which named and shamed organisations that have delivered truly appalling service to me. Memorable customer experiences where I found myself pulling my hair out in despair, disbelief and unbridled frustration.

While these stories have become part of my social repertoire (it's a great party game, called, 'The worst experience I've ever had as a customer'), retelling these stories would be cathartic for me, but somewhat formulaic and repetitive for the reader.

We all know some of the reasons why so many businesses deliver poor service:

- They don't really care.
- They don't employ people who care.
- They don't train or pay their people properly.
- They don't listen.
- They are more interested in their own system.
- They don't mind being mediocre.
- They don't engage their brains.

Personally, it drives me mad. Surely, it is easier to care than to not care – it takes more effort to be rude and uncaring than to be helpful.

Whom do you take your hat off to? Do people take their hat off to you?

Bibliography

Abraham, J, *Getting Everything You Can Out Of Everything You've Got*, Piatkus, 2001.

Barrow, P, *The Bottom Line*, Virgin, 2001.

Bedbury, S and Fenichell, S, *A New Brand World*, Viking Press, 2002.

Craven, RS, *Kick-Start Your Business*, Virgin, 2001.

Cumming, T, *Little e, Big Commerce*, Virgin, 2001.

Daffy, C, *Once a Customer, Always a Customer*, Oaktree Press, 1999.

Dickinson, P, *It's Not About Size*, Virgin, 2001.

Dobbins, R and Pettman, BO, *The Ultimate Entrepreneur's Book*, Capstone, 1999.

Gilbert, A, *Go MAD*, Go Mad Books, 1999.

Godin, S, *Permission Marketing*, Simon & Schuster, 2000.

Godin, S, *Unleashing the Ideavirus*, Hyperion, 2000.

Grant, J, *The New Marketing Manifesto*, Texere, 1999.

Hall, D, *In the Company of Heroes*, Kogan Page, 1999.

Hall, D, *Doing the Business*, Virgin, 2002.

Klein, N, *No Logo*, Flamingo, 2000.

Koch, R, *The 80/20 Principle*, Nicholas Brealey, 1996.

LeBoeuf, M, *How to Win Customers & Keep Them for Life*, Berkeley, 2000.

Levinson, JC, *Guerrilla Marketing Excellence: The 50 Golden Rules for Small Business Success*, Houghton Mifflin, 1992.

Maister, DH, *Managing the Professional Service Firm*, Simon & Schuster, 1997.

McKenna, R, *Relationship Marketing*, Century Business, 1991.

Nordstrom, K and Ridderstrale, J, *Funky Business*, FT Prentice Hall, 2001.

Peters, T, *The Circle of Innovation*, Hodder and Stoughton, 1998.

Porros, JI and Collins, JC, *Built To Last*, Random House, 1994.

Ries, A and Trout, J, *22 Immutable Laws of Marketing*, HarperCollins, 1994.

Rosen, E, *The Anatomy of Buzz*, Currency, 2000.

Sealey, P, *Simplicity Marketing*, Simon & Schuster, 2000.

Treacy, M and Wiersema, F, *The Discipline of Market Leaders*, HarperCollins, 1995.

Wiersema, F, *Customer Intimacy*, HarperCollins, 1998.

Wolff, J, *Do Something Different*, Virgin, 2001.

Glossary |

(a set of loose definitions as they have been applied in the book)

Assets: Anything that is owned by the organisation and is leveraged to produce a profit.

Assumptions: Created when we lack facts, but they are based on previous experience.

Balanced Business Scorecard: A simple technique for assessing your goals and evaluating achievement – it puts strategy (not finance) at the centre of the organisation.

Balance sheet: A snapshot of what the company owns and what it owes.

Barriers to entry: Obstacles making it difficult or impossible for competitors to enter a particular business segment or market.

Barriers to exit: Undesirable forces that keep too many competitors in a market and lead to overcapacity and low profitability because it is thought to be too expensive to leave.

Benchmarking: Identifying the best performers in the marketplace and comparing your own performance indicators with theirs.

BHAG: Big Hairy Audacious Goal.

Brand: The identity given to a product or corporation through its name and design. A name, term, sign, symbol or design, or a combination of these, intended to identify the goods or services of one seller or group of sellers and to differentiate them from those of competitors.

Brand equity: The value of a brand, based on the extent to which it has brand loyalty, name awareness, perceived quality, strong brand associations and other assets such as patents, trademarks and channel relationships.

Business life cycle: The development of a business over a period of time from growth to maturity and then to decline.

Business plan: A comprehensive written statement detailing where the business is going and how it is going to get there.

Business process reengineering: Redesigning a company's processes from first principles to improve costs.

Capital employed: The total amount of funds used within the business.

Category killer: A modern breed of exceptionally aggressive 'off-price' retailers who offer branded merchandise in clearly defined categories at heavily discounted prices.

CEO: Chief executive officer.

Client: A client receives a service and usually pays for it after they have received it – e.g. getting a service from an accountant (compare customer below).

Competitive advantage: The advantage you have over your rivals – when one player has identified a market or market niche where it is possible to have a price and/or cost advantage over its competitors.

Consumer: While the customer/client pays for the product/service, the consumer actually uses it (e.g. the training manager is the client but staff are the consumers).

CSF: Core success factor.

Culture: Shared beliefs, attitudes, values and assumptions within an organisation. How you do things.

Culture audit: An analysis of the way the culture affects the organisation.

Customer: A customer buys a product – they usually pay for it before they receive it (e.g. at a supermarket).

Differentiation: What makes you different from your competitors.

Director: One who directs and/or leads a business.

80:20 Rule: Pareto's Principle, which states that, in most cases, 20 per cent of inputs generate 80 per cent of outputs – the rule of the vital few and the trivial many.

Entrepreneur: Risk taker who identifies opportunities/gaps in the market, and marshals resources to exploit them.

Entrepreneurship: The process of risk taking.

FD: Finance director.

FiMO: Framework for evaluating business performance to date. It stands for finance, marketing and operations. (See *Kick-Start Your Business*).

Four Ps of marketing: Framework for evaluating marketing strategy: product, place, promotion and price.

Glass ceiling: Point of no further upward movement.

Gross profit (GP): Total amount of profit after direct costs, but before overheads.

Human resource management (HRM): The treatment of your people as a valuable asset.

Innovation: The taking of new ideas (products or processes) and making them happen.

Just in time (JIT): Japanese concept that seeks to reduce stock and have components delivered as and when they are needed.

Lifetime value of a customer: How much a customer is actually worth to your business over the time that they might be with you (i.e. not just for the coming year).

Liquidity: The availability of cash.

Manager: One who manages or supervises other people.

Marginal cost: The additional direct cost of producing one extra unit.

Marketing: The concept of identifying and satisfying customers wants and needs profitably.

Market segment: A group of (potential/existing) customers who have common characteristics.

Market share: Percentage of buyers of a product or service who choose your company.

MBA: Master in Business Administration. A university business qualification.

MD: Managing director.

Mission: The numbers that reflect the vision of the business (e.g. turnover, number of employees and profit).

Mission statement: A document that details the company's strategic goals in numbers.

MORFA: A framework for evaluating a business proposition or plan – markets, objectives, resources, financials, ability.

NED: Nonexecutive director.

Net profit: The amount of profit after direct costs and overheads have been deducted.

NLP (neurolinguistic programming): The study of how languages and paralanguage affect thinking and behaviour.

Opt-in: The ability to sign up to join a programme.

Opt-out: The ability to sign out of a programme (to leave it).

Paradigm: A framework of ideas; a pattern or model.

Permission marketing: Getting people to 'buy in' to being involved in your marketing campaign.

Porter's Five Forces: A structural analysis of the market looking at the threat of potential new entrants, the threat from substitutes using different technologies, bargaining power of customers, bargaining power of suppliers and competition among existing suppliers.

Positioning: A market position for a product or a company that separates it from the competitors.

RECoIL: A framework for looking at an organisation's capability to grow: it stands for resources, experience, controls and systems, ideas and innovation and leadership. (See *Kick-Start Your Business.*)

Relationship marketing: The concept of maximising long-term profitability through the intelligent use of information. The information is used to enhance and to create superior relationships with customers.

ROCE (return on capital employed): The return on capital spent within an organisation.

SBU: Strategic business unit – a profit centre within a large firm that can be treated as an autonomous unit.

SME: Small- to medium-sized enterprise typically employing fewer than 200 people.

Spam: Unsolicited emails.

Strategy: Planning that is done in the light of the business environment.

SWOT analysis: Analysis of a company's strengths, weaknesses, opportunities and threats.

TMS: Target market segment.

USP: Unique selling point (or proposition).

Vicious cycle: A continuously reinforcing downward cycle of events.

Viral marketing: The concept of getting your message to spread like a virus via hosts.

Virtuous cycle: A continuously reinforcing upward cycle of events.

Vision: Where you would like the company to be; a blue-skies statement; an inspiring view of what the business could become.

Vision statement: A clear statement of where the company is going.

Working capital: Cash, accounts receivable and stocks.

Zero-based budgeting: Setting budgets afresh, as if the company were a new start-up.

Index

About the Author

Robert Craven spent five years running training and consultancy programmes for entrepreneurial businesses at Warwick Business School. Running his own consultancy since 1998, he is now one of the UK's best-known and sought-after speakers on entrepreneurship. He is not full of theoretical rhetoric: he offers practical solutions – tangible business results.

Craven's work on marketing and strategy has been widely published and acted upon by thousands of growing businesses – he has been described as 'one of the UK's leading marketing specialists' and 'Mr Entrepreneur'.

Craven's track record in helping businesses is very impressive. Add to this his broad experience at board level and you will understand how and why he uniquely adds value to all the businesses that he works with.

Alongside his numerous speaking engagements, Craven also does consulting work for, and is personal coach to, the leaders of a number of growing businesses in the UK.

Craven runs the Directors' Centre Ltd, which provides consultancy and coaching for growth-minded companies. He can be contacted at rc@robert-craven.com or 00 44 (0)1225 851044. Or go to his website at www.robert-craven.com.

CENTRE FOR SMALL & MEDIUM SIZED ENTERPRISES

Warwick is one of a handful of European business schools that have won a truly global reputation. Its high standards of both teaching and research are regularly confirmed by independent ratings and assessments.

The Centre for Small & Medium Sized Enterprises (CSME) is one of the school's major research centres. We have been working with people starting a business, or already running one, since 1985. The Centre also helps established companies to reignite the entrepreneurial flame that is essential for any modern business.

We don't tell entrepreneurs what to do – just help them be more aware and better informed of the opportunities and pitfalls of running a growing small enterprise.

Much of our practical knowledge is gleaned from the experience of individuals who themselves have been there and done it. These kinds of business coaches rarely commit their observations to paper, but in this Virgin/Warwick series they have captured in print their passion and their knowledge. It's a new kind of business publishing that addresses the constantly evolving challenge of business today.

For more information about Warwick Business School (courses, owner networks and other support to entrepreneurs, managers and new enterprises), please contact:

Centre for Small & Medium Sized Enterprises
Warwick Business School
University of Warwick
Coventry
CV4 7AL
UK
Tel: +44 (0) 2476 523741 (CSME); or 524306 (WBS)
Fax: +44(0) 2476 523747 (CSME); or 523719 (WBS)
Email: enquiries@wbs.warwick.ac.uk
And visit CSME's partner website, the Mercia Institute of Enterprise via www.merciainstitute.com
Tel: +44 (0) 2476 574002

Also available in the Virgin Business Guides series:

KICK-START YOUR BUSINESS
100 DAYS TO A LEANER, FITTER ORGANISATION

Robert Craven

Feel your business could do with a tune-up, but are too busy running it to sort out the problems? With the fast, proven techniques in this book, you can transform your workplace into a powerhouse. The case studies, worksheets and practical exercises will help you to take the pain out of business planning, increase your profitability and keep your customers. You'll find out how to identify your company's strengths and weaknesses and assess its potential, and learn the secret obsessions of all successful entrepreneurs.

ISBN 0 7535 0973 3

THE BEST-LAID BUSINESS PLANS
HOW TO WRITE THEM, HOW TO PITCH THEM

Paul Barrow

Planning is not just for start-ups – it's the key to successful business development and growth for every company, new or old. But, once a business is up and running, it's all too easy to concentrate only on day-to-day operations. If you're launching new products and services, taking on more people, relocating to bigger premises, buying a business or selling one, you'll do it better if you plan it. This book shows you how to present the right plan for the right audience – so you stand a better chance of getting what you need. The sound practical advice, case studies and exercises will help you through the planning process and ensure that yours are indeed the best-laid plans.

ISBN 0 7535 0963 6

DO SOMETHING DIFFERENT
PROVEN MARKETING TECHNIQUES TO TRANSFORM YOUR BUSINESS

Jurgen Wolff

If you carry on doing what you've been doing, you'll carry on getting what you've been getting. So, if you want more business, you'd better *Do Something Different*! This book, built around 100 instructive and revealing case studies, contains plenty of advice on how to take charge of your situation and create your own alternatives. It's full of examples of entrepreneurs who took a sideways look at the market and their competitors and decided to branch out and do something a little bit surprising. As a result they made their products and their companies stand out among the competition – vital in today's business environment. Engagingly written by a great individualist, *Do Something Different* will show you how to break the mould and find your way to greater success. Follow its advice and you can set yourself apart from the crowd.

ISBN 0 7535 0993 8

THE BOTTOM LINE
BUSINESS FINANCE: YOUR QUESTIONS ANSWERED

Paul Barrow

'My business is growing and profitable but how come it is always so short of cash?', 'Is it true that I could need nearly half my annual turnover just to fund my debtors and stock – and why?' The answers to these and other frequently asked questions are provided in short, easy to read and understandable sections. These are followed by case studies, giving short insights into what other businesses have done and why it worked for them. Covering topics such as: understanding financial statements; financial analysis and control; break even analysis; profit improvement; securing the right type of funding; and buying and selling a business; *The Bottom Line* is invaluable for those running or managing a business.

ISBN 0 7535 0998 9

PR POWER
INSIDE SECRETS FROM THE WORLD OF SPIN

Amanda Barry

Taking charge of how, when and where to communicate with your customers can make or break your business. Good PR can help you; bad PR can destroy you. Whether you're just starting out or have been in business for years, it's never too late to start harnessing the incredible power of public relations. Drawing on her own experiences and guiding you around the pitfalls, Amanda Barry uses practical hints and tips, toolkit exercises, case studies from real businesses and gives the reader priceless advice from leading experts in PR to show how to get the most from your PR consultancy or in-house team and what to do if you're running the PR yourself.

ISBN 0 7535 0904 0

DOING THE BUSINESS
BOOST YOUR COMPANY'S FORTUNES
David Hall

ISBN 0 7535 0680 7

IT'S NOT ABOUT SIZE
BIGGER BRANDS FOR SMALLER BUSINESSES
Paul Dickinson

ISBN 0 7535 0593 2

20/20 HINDSIGHT
FROM STARTING UP TO SUCCESSFUL ENTREPRENEUR, BY
THOSE WHO'VE BEEN THERE
Rachelle Thackray

ISBN 0 7535 0547 9

LITTLE e, BIG COMMERCE
HOW TO MAKE A PROFIT ONLINE
Timothy Cumming

ISBN 0 7535 0542 8